Anarchism

ANARCHISM
From Theory to Practice
by Daniel Guérin
Introduction by Noam Chomsky
Translated by Mary Klopper

(MR)
Monthly Review Press
New York and London

Contents

Introduction
by Noam Chomsky

A French writer, sympathetic to anarchism, wrote in the 1890's that "anarchism has a broad back, like paper it endures anything" —including, he noted, those whose acts are such that "a mortal enemy of anarchism could not have done better." [1] There have been many styles of anarchist thought and action. It would be hopeless to try to encompass all of these conflicting tendencies in some general theory or ideology. And even if we proceed to extract from the history of libertarian thought a living, evolving tradition, as Daniel Guérin does in the present work, it remains difficult to formulate its doctrines as a specific and determinate theory of society and social change. The anarchist historian Rudolf Rocker, who presents a systematic conception of the development of anarchist thought toward anarcho-syndicalism, along lines that bear comparison to Guérin's work, puts the matter well when he writes that anarchism is not

> a fixed, self-enclosed social system but rather a definite trend in the historic development of mankind, which, in contrast with the intellectual guardianship of all clerical and governmental institutions, strives for the free unhindered unfolding of all the individual and social forces in life. Even freedom is only a relative, not an absolute concept, since it tends constantly to become broader and to affect wider circles in more manifold ways. For the anarchist, freedom is not an abstract philosophical concept, but the vital concrete possibility for every human being to bring to full development all the powers, capacities, and talents with which nature has endowed him, and turn them to social account. The less this natural development of man is influenced by ecclesiastical or political guardianship, the more efficient and harmonious will human personality become, the more will it become the measure of the intellectual culture of the society in which it has grown.[2]

One might ask what value there is in studying a "definite trend in the historic development of mankind" that does not articulate a specific and detailed social theory. Indeed, many commentators dismiss anarchism as utopian, formless, primitive, or otherwise incompatible with the realities of a complex society. One might, however, argue rather differently: that at every stage of history our concern must be to dismantle those forms of authority and oppression that survive from an era when they might have been justified in terms of the need for security or survival or economic development, but that now contribute to—rather than alleviate—material and cultural deficit. If so, there will be no doctrine of social change fixed for the present and future, nor even, necessarily, a specific and unchanging concept of the goals toward which social change should tend. Surely our understanding of the nature of man or of the range of viable social forms is so rudimentary that any far-reaching doctrine must be treated with great skepticism, just as skepticism is in order when we hear that "human nature" or "the demands of efficiency" or "the complexity of modern life" require this or that form of oppression and autocratic rule.

Nevertheless, at a particular time there is every reason to develop, insofar as our understanding permits, a specific realization of this definite trend in the historic development of mankind, appropriate to the tasks of the moment. For Rocker, "the problem that is set for our time is that of freeing man from the curse of economic exploitation and political and social enslavement"; and the method is not the conquest and exercise of state power, or stultifying parliamentarianism, but rather "to reconstruct the economic life of the peoples from the ground up and build it up in the spirit of Socialism":

> But only the producers themselves are fitted for this task, since they are the only value-creating element in society out of which a new future can arise. Theirs must be the task of freeing labor from all the fetters which economic exploitation has fastened on it, of freeing society from all the institutions and procedures of political power, and of opening the way to an alliance of free groups of men and women based on co-operative labor and a planned administration of things in the interest of the community. To prepare the toiling masses in city and country for this great

goal and to bind them together as a militant force is the objective of modern anarch-syndicalism, and in this its whole purpose is exhausted.

As a socialist, Rocker would take for granted "that the serious, final, complete liberation of the workers is only possible on one condition: the appropriation of capital, that is, raw materials and all the tools of labor, including land, by the whole body of workers" (Bakunin). As an anarcho-syndicalist, he insists, further, that the workers' organizations create "not only the ideas but also the facts of the future itself" (Bakunin) in the pre-revolutionary period, that they embody in themselves the structure of the future society—and he looks forward to a social revolution that will dismantle the state apparatus as well as expropriate the expropriators. "What we put in place of the government is industrial organization":

> Anarcho-syndicalists are convinced that a Socialist economic order cannot be created by the decrees and statutes of a government, but only by the solidaric collaboration of the workers with hand and brain in each special branch of production; that is, through the taking over of the management of all plants by the producers themselves under such form that the separate groups, plants, and branches of industry are independent members of the general economic organism and systematically carry on production and the distribution of the products in the interest of the community on the basis of free mutual agreements.

Engels, in a letter of 1883, expressed his disagreement with this conception as follows:

> The anarchists put the thing upside down. They declare that the proletarian revolution must *begin* by doing away with the political organization of the state . . . But to destroy it at such a moment would be to destroy the only organism by means of which the victorious proletariat can assert its newly conquered power, hold down its capitalist adversaries, and carry out that economic revolution of society without which the whole victory must end in a new defeat and in a mass slaughter of the workers similar to those after the Paris Commune.

In contrast, the anarchists—most eloquently Bakunin—warned of the dangers of the "red bureaucracy," that would prove to be "the most vile and terrible lie that our century has created." The anarcho-syndicalist Fernand Pelloutier asked: "Must even the transitory state to which we have to submit necessarily and fatally be the collectivist jail? Can't it consist in a free organization limited exclusively by the needs of production and consumption, all political institutions having disappeared?"

I do not pretend to know the answer to this question. But it seems tolerably clear that unless there is, in some form, a positive answer, the chances for a truly democratic revolution that will achieve the humanistic ideals of the Left are not great. Martin Buber put the problem succinctly when he wrote: "One cannot in the nature of things expect a little tree that has been turned into a club to put forth leaves." The question of conquest or destruction of state power is what Bakunin saw as the primary issue dividing him from Marx.[3] In one form or another, the problem has arisen repeatedly in the century since, dividing "libertarian" from "authoritarian" socialists.

If one were to seek a single dominant idea, within the anarchist tradition, that might be defined as "libertarian socialist," it should, I believe, be that expressed by Bakunin when in writing on the Paris Commune, he identified himself as follows:

> I am a fanatic lover of liberty, considering it as the unique condition under which intelligence, dignity, and human happiness can develop and grow; not the purely formal liberty conceded, measured out, and regulated by the State, an eternal lie which in reality represents nothing more than the privilege of some founded on the slavery of the rest; not the individualistic, egoistic, shabby, and fictitious liberty extolled by the school of J-J. Rousseau and the other schools of bourgeois liberalism, which considers the would-be rights of all men, represented by the State which limits the rights of each—an idea that leads inevitably to the reduction of the rights of each to zero. No, I mean the only kind of liberty that is worthy of the name, liberty that consists in the full development of all the material, intellectual, and moral powers that are latent in each person; liberty that recognizes no restrictions other than those determined by the laws of our own individual nature, which cannot properly be regarded as restrictions since these

laws are not imposed by any outside legislator beside or above us, but are immanent and inherent, forming the very basis of our material, intellectual, and moral being—they do not limit us but are the real and immediate conditions of our freedom.[4]

These ideas grow out of the Enlightenment; their roots are in Rousseau's *Discourse on Inequality*, Humboldt's *Limits of State Action*, Kant's insistence, in his defense of the French Revolution, that freedom is the precondition for acquiring the maturity for freedom, not a gift to be granted when such maturity is achieved. With the development of industrial capitalism, a new and unanticipated system of injustice, it is libertarian socialism that has preserved and extended the radical humanist message of the enlightenment and the classical liberal ideals that were perverted into an ideology to sustain the emerging social order.

In fact, on the very same assumption that led classical liberalism to oppose the intervention of the State in social life, capitalist social relations are also intolerable. Humboldt, for example, in work which anticipated and perhaps inspired Mill, objects to state action because the State tends to "make man an instrument to serve its arbitrary ends, overlooking his individual purposes." He insists that "whatever does not spring from a man's free choice . . . does not enter into his very being, but remains alien to his true nature; he does not perform it with truly human energies, but merely with mechanical exactness." Under the conditions of freedom, "all peasants and craftsmen might be elevated into artists; that is, men who love their own labor for its own sake, improve it by their own plastic genius and inventive skill, and thereby cultivate their intellect, ennoble their character, and exalt and refine their pleasures." When a man merely reacts to external demands and authority, "we may admire what he does, but we despise what he is." Humboldt is, furthermore, no primitive individualist. He summarizes his leading ideas as follows: "While they would break all fetters in human society, they would attempt to find as many new social bonds as possible. The isolated man is no more able to develop than the one who is fettered." This classic of liberal thought, completed in 1792, is in its essence profoundly, though prematurely, anti-capitalist. Its ideas must be attenuated beyond recognition to be transmuted into an ideology of industrial capitalism.

The vision of a society in which social fetters are replaced by social bonds and labor is freely undertaken suggests the early Marx, with his discussion of the "alienation of labor when work is external to the worker . . . not part of his nature . . . [so that] he does not fulfill himself in his work but denies himself . . . [and is] . . . physically exhausted and mentally debased," that alienated labor that "casts some of the workers back into a barbarous kind of work and turns others into machines," thus depriving man of his "species character" of "free conscious activity" and "productive life." It is true that classical libertarian thought is opposed to state intervention in social life, as a consequence of deeper assumptions about human nature and the need for liberty, diversity, and free association. On the same assumptions, capitalist relations of production, wage-slavery, alienated labor, competitiveness, the ideology of "possessive individualism"—all must be regarded as fundamentally anti-human. Libertarian socialism is properly to be regarded as the inheritor of the liberal ideals of the Enlightenment.

Rudolf Rocker describes modern anarchism as "the confluence of the two great currents which during and since the French Revolution have found such characteristic expression in the intellectual life of Europe: Socialism and Liberalism." The classical liberal ideals, he argues, were wrecked on the realities of capitalist economic forms. Anarchism is necessarily anti-capitalist in that it "opposes the exploitation of man by man." But anarchism also opposes "the dominion of man over man." It insists that "*socialism will be free or it will not be at all. In its recognition of this lies the genuine and profound justification for the existence of anarchism.*" From this point of view, anarchism may be regarded as the libertarian wing of socialism. It is in this spirit that Daniel Guérin has approached the study of anarchism in this and other works.[5]

Guérin quotes Adolph Fischer, who said that "every anarchist is a socialist but not every socialist is necessarily an anarchist." Similarly Bakunin, in his "anarchist manifesto" of 1865, the program of his projected international revolutionary fraternity, laid down the principle that each member must be, to begin with, a socialist.]

Any consistent anarchist must oppose private ownership of the means of production and the wage-slavery which is a component of this system, as incompatible with the principle that labor must be freely undertaken and under the control of the producer. As Marx put it, socialists look forward to a society in which labor will "become not only a means of life, but also the highest want in life," an impossibility when the worker is driven by external authority or need rather than inner impulse. A consistent anarchist must oppose not only alienated labor but also the stupefying specialization of labor that takes place when the means for developing production

> mutilate the worker into a fragment of a human being, degrade him to become a mere appurtenance of the machine, make his work such a torment that its essential meaning is destroyed; estrange from him the intellectual potentialities of the labor process in very proportion to the extent to which science is incorporated into it as an independent power . . .[6]

Private ownership of the means of production is, in Proudhon's often-quoted phrase, merely a form of "theft"; it is "the exploitation of the weak by the strong."

In his inevitable attack on the right of private ownership of the means of production,[the anarchist takes his stand with those who struggle to bring about "the third and last emancipatory phase of history," the first having made slaves out of serfs, the second having made wage earners out of serfs, and the third which abolishes the proletariat in a final act of liberation that creates free and voluntary associations of producers](Fourier, 1848).[7] The imminent danger to "civilization" was noted by that perceptive observer, de Tocqueville, also in 1848:

> As long as the right of property was the origin and groundwork of many other rights, it was easily defended—or rather it was not attacked; it was then the citadel of society while all the other rights were its outworks; it did not bear the brunt of attack and, indeed, there was no serious attempt to assail it. But today, when the right of property is regarded as the last undestroyed remnant of the

aristocratic world, when it alone is left standing, the sole privilege in an equalized society, it is a different matter. Consider what is happening in the hearts of the working-classes, although I admit they are quiet as yet. It is true that they are less inflamed than formerly by political passions properly speaking; but do you not see that their passions, far from being political, have become social? Do you not see that, little by little, ideas and opinions are spreading amongst them which aim not merely at removing such and such laws, such a ministry or such a government, but a breaking up the very foundations of society itself? [8]

The workers of Paris, in 1870, broke the silence, and proceeded

to abolish property, the basis of all civilization! Yes, gentlemen, the Commune intended to abolish that class property which makes the labor of the many the wealth of the few. It aimed at the expropriation of the expropriators. It wanted to make individual property a truth by transforming the means of production, land and capital, now chiefly the means of enslaving and exploiting labor, into mere instruments of free and associated labor.

The Commune, of course, was drowned in blood. The nature of the "civilization" that the workers of Paris sought to overcome in their attack on "the very foundations of society itself" was revealed, once again, when the troops of the Versailles government reconquered Paris from its population. As Marx wrote, bitterly but accurately:

The civilization and justice of bourgeois order comes out in its lurid light whenever the slaves and drudges of that order rise against their masters. Then this civilization and justice stand forth as undisguised savagery and lawless revenge . . . the infernal deeds of the soldiery reflect the innate spirit of that civilization of which they are the mercenary vindicators . . . The bourgeoisie of the whole world, which looks complacently upon the wholesale massacre after the battle, is convulsed by horror at the desecration of brick and mortar.[9]

Despite the violent destruction of the Commune, Bakunin wrote that Paris opens a new era, "that of the definitive and complete emancipation of the popular masses and their future true solidarity, across and despite state boundaries . . . the next revolution of man, international and in solidarity, will be the resurrection of Paris"—a revolution that the world still awaits.

[The consistent anarchist, then, will be a socialist, but a socialist of a particular sort. He will not only oppose alienated and specialized labor and look forward to the appropriation of capital by the whole body of workers, but he will also insist that this appropriation be direct, not exercised by some élite force acting in the name of the proletariat. He will, in short, oppose

> the organization of production by the government. It means state socialism, the command of the State officials over production and the command of managers, scientists, shop officials in the shop . . . The goal of the working class is liberation from exploitation. This goal is not reached and cannot be reached by a new directing and governing class substituting itself for the bourgeoisie. [It is only realized by the workers themselves being master over production.]

These remarks are taken from "Five Theses on the Class Struggle" by the left-wing Marxist Anton Pannekoek, one of the outstanding theorists of the Council Communist movement. And in fact, radical Marxism merges with anarchist currents.

As a further illustration, consider the following characterization of "revolutionary socialism":

> The revolutionary Socialist denies that State ownership can end in anything other than a bureaucratic despotism. We have seen why the State cannot democratically control industry. Industry can only be democratically owned and controlled by the workers electing directly from their own ranks industrial administrative committees. Socialism will be fundamentally an industrial system; its constituencies will be of an industrial character. Thus those carrying on the social activities and industries of society will be directly represented in the local and central councils of social administration. In this way the powers of such delegates will flow upwards from those carrying on the work and conversant with the needs of the community. When the central administrative industrial committee meets it will represent every phase of social activity. Hence the capitalist political or geographical state will be replaced by the industrial administrative committee of Socialism. The transition from the one social system to the other will be the *social revolution*.

The political State throughout history has meant the government *of men* by ruling classes; the Republic of Socialism will be the government *of industry* administered on behalf of the whole community. The former meant the economic and political subjection of the many; the latter will mean the economic freedom of all—it will be, therefore, a true democracy.

These remarks are taken from William Paul's *The State, its Origins and Function,* written in early 1917 [10]—shortly before Lenin's *State and Revolution,* perhaps his most libertarian work. Paul was a member of the Marxist–De Leonist Socialist Labor Party, and was later one of the founders of the British Communist Party.[11] His critique of state socialism resembles the libertarian doctrine of the anarchists in its principle that since state ownership and management will lead to bureaucratic despotism, the social revolution must replace it by the industrial organization of society with direct workers' control. Many similar statements can be cited.

What is far more important is that these ideas have been realized in spontaneous revolutionary action, for example in Germany and Italy after World War I and in Spain (specifically, industrial Barcelona) in 1936. One might argue that some form of council communism is the natural form of revolutionary socialism in an industrial society. It reflects the intuitive understanding that democracy is largely a sham when the industrial system is controlled by any form of autocratic élite, whether of owners, managers and technocrats, a "vanguard" party, or a state bureaucracy. Under these conditions of authoritarian domination the classical liberal ideals developed further by Marx and Bakunin and all true revolutionaries cannot be realized; man will not be free to develop his own potentialities to their fullest, and the producer will remain "a fragment of a human being," degraded, a tool in the productive process directed from above.

The ideas of libertarian socialism, in this sense, have been submerged in the industrial societies of the past half-century. The dominant ideologies have been those of state socialism or state capitalism (in the United States, of an increasingly militarized character, for reasons that are not obscure[12]). But there has been a resurgence in the past few years. The theses I quoted by Anton Pannekoek were taken from a recent pamphlet of a radical French workers' group (*Informations Correspondance Ouvrière*). The quotation from William Paul on revolutionary socialism appears in a paper by Walter Kendall given at the National Conference on Workers' Control in Sheffield, England, in March 1969. The workers' control movement has become a significant force in England in the past few years. It has organized several conferences, has produced a substantial pamphlet literature, and counts among its active adherents representatives of some of the most important trade unions. The Amalgamated Engineering and Foundryworkers' Union, for example, has adopted, as official policy, the program of nationalization of basic industries under "workers' control at all levels." [13] On the continent, there are similar developments. May 1968, of course accelerated the growing interest in council communism and related ideas in France and Germany, as it did in England.

Given the general conservative cast of our highly ideological society, it is not too surprising that the United States has been relatively untouched by these developments, but that too may change. The erosion of the Cold War mythology at least makes it possible to raise these questions in fairly broad circles. If the present wave of repression can be beaten back, if the Left can overcome its more suicidal tendencies and build upon what has been accomplished in the past decade, then the problem of how to organize industrial society on truly democratic lines, with democratic control in the work place and in the community, should become a dominant intellectual issue for those who are alive to the problems of contemporary society, and, as a mass movement for libertarian socialism develops, speculation should proceed to action.

In his manifesto of 1865, Bakunin predicted that one element in the social revolution will be "that intelligent and truly noble part of the youth which, though belonging by birth to the privileged classes, in its generous convictions and ardent aspirations, adopts the cause of the people." Perhaps in the rise of the student movement of the 1960's one sees the beginnings of a fulfillment of this prophecy.

Daniel Guérin has undertaken what he describes elsewhere as a "process of rehabilitation" of anarchism. He argues, convincingly I believe, that "the constructive ideas of anarchism retain their vitality, that they may, when re-examined and sifted, assist contemporary socialist thought to undertake a new departure . . . [and] . . . contribute to enriching Marxism." [14] From the "broad back" of anarchism he has selected for more intensive scrutiny those ideas and actions that can be described as libertarian socialist. This is natural and proper. This framework accommodates the major anarchist spokesmen as well as the mass actions that have been animated by anarchist sentiments and ideals. Guérin is concerned not only with anarchist thought but also with the spontaneous actions of popular forces that actually create new social forms in the course of revolutionary struggle. He is concerned with social as well as intellectual creativity. Furthermore, he attempts to draw from the constructive achievements of the past lessons that will enrich the theory of social liberation. For those who wish not only to understand the world, but also to change it, this is the proper way to study the history of anarchism.

Guérin describes the anarchism of the nineteenth century as essentially doctrinal, while the twentieth century, for the anarchists, has been a time of "revolutionary practice." [15] The present work reflects that judgment. His interpretation of anarchism consciously points toward the future. Arthur Rosenberg once noted that popular revolutions characteristically seek to replace "a feudal or centralized authority ruling by force" with some form of communal system which "implies the destruction and disappearance of the old form of State." Such a system will either be socialist or an "extreme form of democracy . . . [which is] . . . the preliminary condition for Socialism inasmuch as Socialism can only be realized in a world enjoying the highest possible measure of individual freedom." This ideal, he notes, was common to Marx and the anarchists.[16] This natural struggle for liberation runs counter to the prevailing tendency toward centralization in economic and political life. A century ago Marx wrote that the workers of Paris "felt there was but one alternative—

the Commune, or the empire—under whatever name it might reappear."

The empire had ruined them economically by the havoc it made of public wealth, by the wholesale financial swindling it fostered, by the props it lent to the artificially accelerated centralization of capital, and the concomitant expropriation of their own ranks. It had suppressed them politically, it had shocked them morally by its orgies, it had insulted their Voltarianism by handing over the education of their children to the *frères Ignorantins*, it had revolted their national feeling as Frenchmen by precipitating them headlong into a war which left only one equivalent for the ruins it made—the disappearance of the empire.[17]

The miserable Second Empire "was the only form of government possible at a time when the bourgeoisie had already lost, and the working class had not yet acquired, the faculty of ruling the nation."

It is not very difficult to rephrase these remarks so that they become appropriate to the imperial systems of 1970. The problem of "freeing man from the curse of economic exploitation and political and social enslavement" remains the problem of our time. As long as this is so, the doctrines and the revolutionary practice of libertarian socialism will serve as an inspiration and a guide.

Notes

1. Octave Mirbeau, quoted in James Joll, *The Anarchists* (Boston, 1964).
2. *Anarcho-syndicalism* (London, 1938).
3. For an informative discussion of the impact of the Paris Commune on this dispute see Daniel Guérin's comments in his excellent historical anthology of the anarchist movement, *Ni Dieu ni Maître* (Lausanne, 1969).
4. "La Commune de Paris et la Notion de l'Etat," in *Ni Dieu ni Maître*.
5. See his *Jeunesse du socialisme libertaire* (Paris, 1959), and *Pour un Marxisme Libertaire* (Paris, 1969).
6. Marx, *Capital*. Quoted by Robert Tucker, who rightly emphasizes that Marx sees the revolutionary more as a "frustrated producer" than a "dissatisfied consumer" (*The Marxian Revolutionary*

Idea [New York, 1969]). This more radical critique of capitalist relations of production is a direct outgrowth of the libertarian thought of the Enlightenment.

7. Cited in Buber's *Paths in Utopia*, 1945; (Boston, 1958).
8. Cited in J. Hampden Jackson, *Marx, Proudhon, and European Socialism* (New York, 1962).
9. Marx, *The Civil War in France*, 1871; (New York, 1940).
10. Socialist Labour Press (Glasgow, nd.).
11. For some background, see Walter Kendall, *The Revolutionary Movement in Britain* (London, 1969).
12. For a good discussion, see Michael Kidron, *Western Capitalism Since the War* (London, 1968).
13. See Hugh Scanlon, "The Way Forward for Workers' Control," Institute for Workers' Control, 91 Goldsmith Street, Nottingham, England. Pamphlet Series No. 1, 1968. Scanlon is the President of the AEF, the second largest trade union in Britain. The Institute was established as a result of the Sixth Conference on Workers' Control, March 1968, and serves as a center for disseminating information and encouraging research.
14. Introduction to *Ni Dieu ni Maître*.
15. *Ibid.*
16. *A History of Bolshevism*, 1932 (New York, 1965).
17. *The Civil War in France*.

Anarchism

Preface

There has recently been a renewal of interest in anarchism. Books, pamphlets, and anthologies are being devoted to it. It is doubtful whether this literary effort is really very effective. It is difficult to trace the outlines of anarchism. Its master thinkers rarely condensed their ideas into systematic works. If, on occasion, they tried to do so, it was only in thin pamphlets designed for propaganda and popularization in which only fragments of their ideas can be observed. Moreover, there are several kinds of anarchism and many variations within the thought of each of the great libertarians.

Rejection of authority and stress on the priority of individual judgment make it natural for libertarians to "profess the faith of antidogmatism." "Let us not become the leaders of a new religion," Proudhon wrote to Marx, "even were it to be the religion of logic and reason." It follows that the views of the libertarians are more varied, more fluid, and harder to apprehend than those of the authoritarian socialists* whose rival churches at least try to impose a set of beliefs on their faithful.

Just before he was sent to the guillotine, the terrorist Emile Henry wrote a letter to the governor of the prison where he was awaiting execution explaining: "Beware of believing anarchy to be a dogma, a doctrine above question or debate, to be venerated by its adepts as is the Koran by devout Moslems. No! the absolute freedom which we demand constantly develops our thinking and

---

* "Authoritarian" was an epithet used by the libertarian anarchists and denoted those socialists whom they considered less libertarian than themselves and who they therefore presumed were in favor of authority.

raises it toward new horizons (according to the turn of mind of various individuals), takes it out of the narrow framework of regulation and codification. We are not 'believers'!" The condemned man went on to reject the "blind faith" of the French Marxists of his period: "They believe something because Guesde* has said one must believe it, they have a catechism and it would be sacrilege to question any of its clauses."

In spite of the variety and richness of anarchist thinking, in spite of contradictions and doctrinal disputes which were often centered on false problems, anarchism presents a fairly homogeneous body of ideas. At first sight it is true that there may seem to be a vast difference between the individualist anarchism of Stirner (1806–1856) and social anarchism. When one looks more deeply into the matter, however, the partisans of total freedom and those of social organization do not appear as far apart as they may have thought themselves, or as others might at first glance suppose. The anarchist *sociétaire*† is also an individualist and the individualist anarchist may well be a partisan of the *sociétaire* approach who fears to declare himself.

The relative unity of social anarchism arises from the fact that it was developed during a single period by two masters, one of whom was the disciple and follower of the other: the Frenchman Pierre-Joseph Proudhon (1809–1865) and the Russian exile Mikhail Bakunin (1814–1876). The latter defined anarchism as "Proudhonism greatly developed and pushed to its furthest conclusion." This type of anarchism called itself collectivist.

Its successors, however, rejected the term and proclaimed themselves to be communists ("libertarian communists," of course). One of them, another Russian exile, Peter Kropotkin (1842–1921), bent the doctrine in a more rigidly utopian and optimistic direction but his "scientific" approach failed to conceal its weaknesses. The Italian Errico Malatesta (1853–1932), on the other hand, turned to audacious and sometimes puerile activism although

---

* Jules Guesde (1845–1922) in 1879 introduced Marxist ideas to the French workers' movement. (Translator's note.)

† The term *sociétaire* is used to define a form of anarchism which repudiates individualism and aims at integration into society. (Translator's note.)

he enriched anarchist thinking with his intransigent and often lucid polemics. Later the experience of the Russian Revolution produced one of the most remarkable anarchist works, that of Voline (1882–1945).*

The anarchist terrorism of the end of the nineteenth century had dramatic and anecdotal features and an aura of blood which appeal to the taste of the general public. In its time it was a school for individual energy and courage, which command respect, and it had the merit of drawing social injustice to public attention; but today it seems to have been a temporary and sterile deviation in the history of anarchism. It seems out-of-date. To fix one's attention on the "stewpot" of Ravachol† is to ignore or underestimate the fundamental characteristics of a definite concept of social reorganization. When this concept is properly studied it appears highly constructive and not destructive, as its opponents pretend. It is this constructive aspect of anarchism that will be presented to the reader in this study. By what right and upon what basis? Because the material studied is not antiquated but relevant to life, and because it poses problems which are more acute than ever. It appears that libertarian thinkers anticipated the needs of our time to a considerable extent.

This small book does not seek to duplicate the histories and bibliographies of anarchism already published. Their authors were scholars, mainly concerned with omitting no names and, fascinated by superficial similarities, they discovered numerous forerunners of anarchism. They gave almost equal weight to the genius and to his most minor follower, and presented an excess of biographical details rather than making a profound study of ideas. Their learned tomes leave the reader with a feeling of diffusion,

---

* "Voline" was the pseudonym of V. M. Eichenbaum, author of *La Révolution Inconnue 1917–1921*, the third volume of which is in English as *The Unknown Revolution* (1955). Another partial translation is *Nineteen-seventeen: The Russian Revolution Betrayed* (1954). (Translator's note.)

 † Alias of the French terrorist François-Claudius Koenigstein (1859–1892) who committed many acts of violent terrorism and was eventually executed. (Translator's note.)

almost incoherence, still asking himself what anarchism really is. I have tried a somewhat different approach. I assume that the lives of the masters of libertarian thought are known. In any case, they are often much less illuminating for our purpose than some writers imagine. Many of these masters were not anarchists throughout their lives and their complete works include passages which have nothing to do with anarchism.

To take an example: in the second part of his career Proudhon's thinking took a conservative turn. His verbose and monumental *De la Justice dans la Révolution et dans l'Eglise* (1858) was mainly concerned with the problem of religion and its conclusion was far from libertarian. In the end, in spite of passionate anti-clericalism, he accepted all the categories of Catholicism, subject to his own interpretations, proclaimed that the instruction and moral training of the people would benefit from the preservation of Christian symbolism, and in his final words seemed almost ready to say a prayer. Respect for his memory inhibits all but a passing reference to his "salute to war," his diatribes against women, or his fits of racism.

The opposite happened to Bakunin. His wild early career as a revolutionary conspirator was unconnected with anarchism. He embraced libertarian ideas only in 1864 after the failure of the Polish insurrection in which he played a part. His earlier writings have no place in an anarchist anthology. As for Kropotkin, his purely scientific work, for which he is today celebrated in the U.S.S.R. as a shining light in the study of national geography, has no more connection with anarchism than had his prowar attitude during the First World War.

In place of a historical and chronological sequence an unusual method has been adopted in this book: the reader will be presented in turn with the main constructive themes of anarchism, and not with personalities. I have intentionally omitted only elements which are not specifically libertarian, such as the critique of capitalism, atheism, antimilitarism, free love, etc. Rather than give secondhand and therefore faded paraphrases unsupported by evidence, I have allowed quotations to speak directly as far as possible. This gives the reader access to the ideas of the masters in their warm and living form, as they were originally penned.

Secondly, the doctrine is examined from a different angle: it is shown in the great periods when it was put to the test by events —the Russian Revolution of 1917, Italy after 1918, the Spanish Revolution of 1936. The final chapter treats what is undoubtedly the most original creation of anarchism: workers' self-management as it has been developed in the grip of contemporary reality, in Yugoslavia and Algeria—and soon, perhaps, who knows, in the U.S.S.R.

Throughout this little book the reader will see two conceptions of socialism contrasted and sometimes related to one another, one authoritarian, the other libertarian. By the end of the analysis it is hoped that the reader will be led to ask himself which is the conception of the future.

1

The Basic Ideas of Anarchism

A MATTER OF WORDS

The word *anarchy* is as old as the world. It is derived from two ancient Greek words, αν (an), αρχη (arkhê), and means something like the absence of authority or government. However, for millennia the presumption has been accepted that man cannot dispense with one or the other, and anarchy has been understood in a pejorative sense, as a synonym for disorder, chaos, and disorganization.

Pierre-Joseph Proudhon was famous for his quips (such as "property is theft") and took to himself the word anarchy. As if his purpose were to shock as much as possible, in 1840 he engaged in the following dialogue with the "Philistine."

"You are a republican."

"Republican, yes; but that means nothing. *Res publica* is 'the State.' Kings, too, are republicans."

"Ah well! You are a democrat?"

"No."

"What! Perhaps you are a monarchist?"

"No."

"Constitutionalist then?"

"God forbid."

"Then you are an aristocrat?"

"Not at all!"

"You want a mixed form of government?"

"Even less."

"Then what are you?"

"An anarchist."

He sometimes made the concession of spelling anarchy "an-archy" to put the packs of adversaries off the scent. By this term he understood anything but disorder. Appearances notwithstanding, he was more constructive than destructive, as we shall see. He held government responsible for disorder and believed that

11

only a society without government could restore the natural order and re-create social harmony. He argued that the language could furnish no other term and chose to restore to the old word anarchy its strict etymological meaning [In the heat of his polemics, however, he obstinately and paradoxically also used the word anarchy in its pejorative sense of disorder, thus making confusion worse confounded.] His disciple Mikhail Bakunin followed him in this respect.

Proudhon and Bakunin carried this even further, taking malicious pleasure in playing with the confusion created by the use of the two opposite meanings of the word: for them, anarchy was both the most colossal disorder, the most complete disorganization of society and, beyond this gigantic revolutionary change, the construction of a new, stable, and rational order based on freedom and solidarity.

The immediate followers of the two fathers of anarchy hesitated to use a word so deplorably elastic, conveying only a negative idea to the uninitiated, and lending itself to ambiguities which could be annoying to say the least. Even Proudhon became more cautious toward the end of his brief career and was happy to call himself a "federalist." His petty-bourgeois descendants preferred the term *mutuellisme* to *anarchisme* and the socialist line adopted *collectivisme*, soon to be displaced by *communisme*. At the end of the century in France, Sébastien Faure took up a word originated in 1858 by one Joseph Déjacque to make it the title of a journal, *Le Libertaire*. Today the terms "anarchist" and "libertarian" have become interchangeable.

Most of these terms have a major disadvantage: they fail to express the basic characteristics of the doctrines they are supposed to describe. Anarchism is really a synonym for socialism. The anarchist is primarily a socialist whose aim is to abolish the exploitation of man by man. Anarchism is only one of the streams of socialist thought, that stream whose main components are concern for liberty and haste to abolish the State. Adolph Fischer, one of the Chicago martyrs,* claimed that "every anarchist is a socialist, but every socialist is not necessarily an anarchist."

---

* In 1883 an active nucleus of revolutionary socialists founded an International Working Men's Association in the United States. They were under

Some anarchists consider themselves to be the best and most logical socialists, but they have adopted a label also attached to the terrorists, or have allowed others to hang it around their necks. This has often caused them to be mistaken for a sort of "foreign body" in the socialist family and has led to a long string of misunderstandings and verbal battles—usually quite purposeless. Some contemporary anarchists have tried to clear up the misunderstanding by adopting a more explicit term: they align themselves with libertarian socialism or communism.

A VISCERAL REVOLT

Anarchism can be described first and foremost as a visceral revolt. The anarchist is above all a man in revolt. He rejects society as a whole along with its guardians. Max Stirner declared that the anarchist frees himself of all that is sacred, and carries out a vast operation of deconsecration. These "vagabonds of the intellect," these "bad characters," "refuse to treat as intangible truths things

---

the influence of the International Anarchist Congress, held in London in 1881, and also of Johann Most, a social democrat turned anarchist, who reached America in 1882. Albert R. Parsons and Adolph Fischer were the moving spirits in the association, which took the lead in a huge mass movement concentrated on winning an eight-hour day. The campaign for this was launched by the trade unions and the Knights of Labor, and May 1, 1886, was fixed as the deadline for bringing the eight-hour day into force. During the first half of May, a nationwide strike involved 190,000 workers, of whom 80,000 were in Chicago. Impressive mass demonstrations occurred in that city on May 1 and for several days thereafter. Panic-stricken and terrified by this wave of rebellion, the bourgeoisie resolved to crush the movement at its source, resorting to bloody provocation if need be. During a street meeting on May 4, 1885, in Haymarket Square, a bomb thrown at the legs of the police in an unexplained manner provided the necessary pretext. Eight leaders of the revolutionary and libertarian socialist movement were arrested, seven of them sentenced to death, and four subsequently hanged (a fifth committed suicide in his cell the day before the execution). Since then the Chicago martyrs—Parsons, Fischer, Engel, Spies, and Lingg—have belonged to the international proletariat, and the universal celebration of May Day (May 1) still commemorates the atrocious crime committed in the United States.

that give respite and consolation to thousands and instead leap
over the barriers of tradition to indulge without restraint the
fantasies of their impudent critique." *

Proudhon rejected all and any "official persons"—philosophers,
priests, magistrates, academicians, journalists, parliamentarians,
etc.—for whom "the people is always a monster to be fought,
muzzled, and chained down; which must be led by trickery like
the elephant or the rhinoceros; or cowed by famine; and which
is bled by colonization and war." Elisée Reclus† explained why
society seems, to these well-heeled gentlemen, worth preserving:
"Since there are rich and poor, rulers and subjects, masters and
servants, Caesars who give orders for combat and gladiators who
go and die, the prudent need only place themselves on the side
of the rich and the masters, and make themselves into courtiers
to the emperors."

His permanent state of revolt makes the anarchist sympathetic
to nonconformists and outlaws, and leads him to embrace the
cause of the convict and the outcast. Bakunin thought that Marx
and Engels spoke most unfairly of the lumpenproletariat, of the
"proletariat in rags": "For the spirit and force of the future social
revolution is with it and it alone, and not with the stratum of the
working class which has become like the bourgeoisie."

Explosive statements which an anarchist would not disavow
were voiced by Balzac through the character of Vautrin, a powerful incarnation of social protest—half rebel, half criminal.

HORROR OF THE STATE

The anarchist regards the State as the most deadly of the pre-
conceptions which have blinded men through the ages. Stirner
denounced him who "throughout eternity . . . is obsessed by the
State."

---

* All quotations have been translated into English by the translator.

† French writer (1830–1905) known principally as a geographer. His brother
Elie played an active part during the Commune of 1871. (Translator's note.)

Proudhon was especially fierce against "this fantasy of our minds that the first duty of a free and rational being is to refer to museums and libraries," and he laid bare the mechanism whereby "this mental predisposition has been maintained and its fascination made to seem invincible: government has always presented itself to men's minds as the natural organ of justice and the protector of the weak." He mocked the inveterate authoritarians who "bow before power like church wardens before the sacrament" and reproached "all parties without exception" for turning their gaze "unceasingly toward authority as if to the polestar." He longed for the day when "renunciation of authority shall have replaced faith in authority and the political catechism."

[Kropotkin jeered at the bourgeois who "regarded the people as a horde of savages who would be useless as soon as government ceased to function."] Malatesta anticipated psychoanalysis when he uncovered the fear of freedom in the subconscious of authoritarians.

What is wrong with the State in the eyes of the anarchists?

Stirner expressed it thus: "We two are enemies, the State and I." "Every State is a tyranny, be it the tyranny of a single man or a group." Every State is necessarily what we now call totalitarian: "The State has always one purpose: to limit, control, subordinate the individual and subject him to the general purpose . . . . Through its censorship, its supervision, and its police the State tries to obstruct all free activity and sees this repression as its duty, because the instinct of self-preservation demands it." "The State does not permit me to use my thoughts to their full value and communicate them to other men . . . unless they are its own. . . . Otherwise it shuts me up."

Proudhon wrote in the same vein: ["The government of man by man is servitude."] "Whoever lays a hand on me to govern me is a usurper and a tyrant. I declare him to be my enemy." He launched into a tirade worthy of a Molière or a Beaumarchais:

> To be governed is to be watched over, inspected, spied on, directed, legislated, regimented, closed in, indoctrinated, preached at, controlled, assessed, evaluated, censored, commanded; all by creatures that have neither the right, nor wisdom, nor virtue. . . . To be governed means that at every move, operation, or transaction one

is noted, registered, entered in a census, taxed, stamped, priced, assessed, patented, licensed, authorized, recommended, admonished, prevented, reformed, set right, corrected. Government means to be subjected to tribute, trained, ransomed, exploited, monopolized, extorted, pressured, mystified, robbed; all in the name of public utility and the general good. Then, at the first sign of resistance or word of complaint, one is repressed, fined, despised, vexed, pursued, hustled, beaten up, garroted, imprisoned, shot, machine-gunned, judged, sentenced, deported, sacrificed, sold, betrayed, and to cap it all, ridiculed, mocked, outraged, and dishonored. *That* is government, *that* is its justice and its morality! . . . O human personality! How can it be that you have cowered in such subjection for sixty centuries?"

Bakunin sees the State as an "abstraction devouring the life of the people," an "immense cemetery where all the real aspirations and living forces of a country generously and blissfully allow themselves to be buried in the name of that abstraction."

According to Malatesta, "far from creating energy, government by its methods wastes, paralyzes, and destroys enormous potential."

As the powers of the State and its bureaucracy widen, the danger grows more acute. Proudhon foresaw the greatest evil of the twentieth century: "*Fonctionnairisme* [legalistic rule by civil servants] . . . leads toward state communism, the absorption of all local and individual life into the administrative machinery, and the destruction of all free thought. Everyone wants to take refuge under the wing of power, to live in common." It is high time to call a halt: "Centralization has grown stronger and stronger . . . , things have reached . . . the point where society and government can no longer coexist." "From the top of the hierarchy to the bottom there is nothing in the State which is not an abuse to be reformed, a form of parasitism to be suppressed, or an instrument of tyranny to be destroyed. And you speak to us of preserving the State, and increasing the power of the State! Away with you—you are no revolutionary!"

Bakunin had an equally clear and painful vision of an increasingly totalitarian State. He saw the forces of world counter-revolution, "based on enormous budgets, permanent armies, and a formidable bureaucracy" and endowed "with all the terrible means of action given to them by modern centralization," as becoming "an immense, crushing, threatening reality."

HOSTILITY TO BOURGEOIS DEMOCRACY

The anarchist denounces the deception of bourgeois democracy even more bitterly than does the authoritarian socialist. The bourgeois democratic State, christened "the nation," does not seem to Stirner any less to be feared than the old absolutist State. "The monarch . . . was a very poor man compared with the new one, the 'sovereign nation.' In liberalism we have only the continuation of the ancient contempt for the Self." "Certainly many privileges have been eliminated through time but only for the benefit of the State . . . and not at all to strengthen my Self."

In Proudhon's view "democracy is nothing but a constitutional tyrant." The people were declared sovereign by a "trick" of our forefathers. In reality they are a monkey king which has kept only the title of sovereign without the magnificence and grandeur. The people rule but do not govern, and delegate their sovereignty through the periodic exercise of universal suffrage, abdicating their power anew every three or five years. The dynasts have been driven from the throne but the royal prerogative has been preserved intact. In the hands of a people whose education has been willfully neglected the ballot is a cunning swindle benefiting only the united barons of industry, trade, and property.

The very theory of the sovereignty of the people contains its own negation. If the entire people were truly sovereign there would no longer be either government or governed; the sovereign would be reduced to nothing; the State would have no *raison d'être*, would be identical with society and disappear into industrial organization.

Bakunin saw that the "representative system, far from being a guarantee for the people, on the contrary, creates and safeguards the continued existence of a governmental aristocracy against the people." Universal suffrage is a sleight of hand, a bait, a safety valve, and a mask behind which "hides the really despotic power of the State based on the police, the banks, and the army," "an excellent way of oppressing and ruining a people in the name of the so-called popular will which serves to camouflage it."

The anarchist does not believe in emancipation by the ballot. Proudhon was an abstentionist, at least in theory, thinking that "the social revolution is seriously compromised if it comes about through the political revolution." To vote would be a contradiction, an act of weakness and complicity with the corrupt regime: "We must make war on all the old parties together, using parliament as a legal battlefield, but staying outside it." "Universal suffrage is the counter-revolution," and to constitute itself a class the proletariat must first "secede from" bourgeois democracy.

However, the militant Proudhon frequently departed from this position of principle. In June 1848 he let himself be elected to parliament and was briefly stuck in the parliamentary glue. On two occasions, during the partial elections of September 1848 and the presidental elections of December 10 of the same year, he supported the candidacy of Raspail, a spokesman of the extreme Left. He even went so far as to allow himself to be blinded by the tactic of the "the lesser evil," expressing a preference for General Cavaignac, persecutor of the Paris proletariat, over the apprentice dictator Louis Napoleon. Much later, in 1863 and 1864, he did advocate returning blank ballot papers, but as a demonstration against the imperial dictatorship, not in opposition to universal suffrage, which he now christened "the democratic principle par excellence."

Bakunin and his supporters in the First International objected to the epithet "abstentionist" hurled at them by the Marxists. For them, boycotting the ballot box was a simple tactical question and not an article of faith. Although they gave priority to the class struggle in the economic field, they would not agree that they ignored "politics." They were not rejecting "politics," but only bourgeois politics. They did not disapprove of a political revolution unless it was to come before the social revolution. They steered clear of other movements only if these were not directed to the immediate and complete emancipation of the workers. What they feared and denounced were ambiguous electoral alliances with radical bourgeois parties of the 1848 type, or "popular fronts," as they would be called today. They also feared that when workers were elected to parliament and translated into bourgeois living conditions, they would cease to be workers and turn into Statesmen, becoming bourgeois, perhaps even more bourgeois than the bourgeoisie itself.

However, the anarchist attitude toward universal suffrage is far from logical or consistent. Some considered the ballot as a last expedient. Others, more uncompromising, regarded its use as damnable in any circumstances and made it a matter of doctrinal purity. Thus, at the time of the *Cartel des Gauches* (Alliance of the Left) elections in May 1924, Malatesta refused to make any concession. He admitted that in certain circumstances the outcome of an election might have "good" or "bad" consequences and that the result would sometimes depend on anarchist votes, especially if the forces of the opposing political groupings were fairly evenly balanced. "But no matter! Even if some minimal progress were to be the direct result of an electoral victory, the anarchist should not rush to the polling stations." He concluded: "Anarchists have always kept themselves pure, and remain the revolutionary party par excellence, the party of the future, because they have been able to resist the siren song of elections."

The inconsistency of anarchist doctrine on this matter was to be especially well illustrated in Spain. In 1930 the anarchists joined in a common front with bourgeois democrats to overthrow the dictator, Primo de Rivera. The following year, despite their official abstention, many went to the polls in the municipal elections which led to the overthrow of the monarchy. In the general election of November 1933 they strongly recommended abstention from voting, and this returned a violently anti-labor Right to power for more than two years. The anarchists had taken care to announce in advance that if their abstention led to a victory for reaction they would launch the social revolution. They soon attempted to do so but in vain and at the cost of heavy losses (dead, wounded, and imprisoned).

When the parties of the Left came together in the Popular Front in 1936, the central anarcho-syndicalist organization was hard pressed to know what attitude to adopt. Finally it declared itself, very halfheartedly, for abstention, but its campaign was so tepid as to go unheard by the masses who were in any case already committed to participation in the elections. By going to the polls the mass of voters insured the triumph of the Popular Front (263 left-wing deputies, as against 181 others).

It should be noted that in spite of their savage attacks on bourgeois democracy, the anarchists admitted that it is relatively progressive. Even Stirner, the most intransigent, occasionally let slip the word "progress." Proudhon conceded: "When a people passes from the monarchical to the democratic State, some progress is made." And Bakunin said: "It should not be thought that we want . . . to criticize the bourgeois government in favor of monarchy. . . . The most imperfect republic is a thousand times better than the most enlightened monarchy. . . . The democratic system gradually educates the masses to public life." This disproves Lenin's view that "some anarchists" proclaim "that the form of oppression is a matter of indifference to the proletariat." This also dispels the fear expressed by Henri Arvon in his little book *L'Anarchisme* that anarchist opposition to democracy could be confused with counter-revolutionary opposition.

❋

CRITIQUE OF AUTHORITARIAN SOCIALISM

The anarchists were unanimous in subjecting authoritarian socialism to a barrage of severe criticism. At the time when they made violent and satirical attacks these were not entirely well founded, for those to whom they were addressed were either primitive or "vulgar" communists, whose thought had not yet been fertilized by Marxist humanism, or else, in the case of Marx and Engels themselves, were not as set on authority and state control as the anarchists made out.

Although in the nineteenth century authoritarian tendencies in socialist thought were still embryonic and undeveloped, they have proliferated in our time. In the face of these excrescences, the anarchist critique seems less tendentious, less unjust; sometimes it even seems to have a prophetic ring.

Stirner accepted many of the premises of communism but with the following qualification: [the profession of communist faith is a first step toward total emancipation of the victims of our society, but they will become completely "disalienated," and truly able to develop their individuality, only by advancing beyond communism.]

As Stirner saw it, in a communist system the worker remains subject to the rule of a society of workers. His work is imposed on him by society, and remains for him a task. Did not the communist Weitling* write: ["Faculties can only be developed in so far as they do not disrupt the harmony of society"?] To which Stirner replied: "Whether I were to be 'loyal' to a tyrant or to Weitling's 'society' I would suffer the same absence of rights."

According to Stirner, the communist does not think of the man behind the worker. He overlooks the most important issue: [to give man the opportunity to enjoy himself as an individual after he has fulfilled his task as a producer.] Above all, Stirner glimpsed the danger that in a communist society the collective appropriation of the means of production would give the State more exorbitant powers than it has at present:

> By abolishing all private property communism makes me even more dependent on others, on the generality or totality [of society], and, in spite of its attacks on the State, it intends to establish its own State, . . . a state of affairs which paralyzes my freedom to act and exerts sovereign authority over me. Communism is rightly indignant about the wrongs which I suffer at the hands of individual proprietors, but the power which it will put into the hands of the total society is even more terrible.

Proudhon was just as dissatisfied with the "governmental, dictatorial, authoritarian, doctrinaire communist system" which "starts from the principle that the individual is entirely subordinate to the collectivity." The communist idea of the State is exactly the same as that of the former masters and much less liberal: "Like an army that has captured the enemy's guns, com-

---

* Wilhelm Weitling (1808–1871), German utopian communist writer and founder of Communist Workers' Clubs during the 1830's and 1840's. (Translator's note.)

munism has simply turned property's artillery against the army of property. The slave always apes his master." And Proudhon describes in the following terms the political system which he attributes to the communists:

> A compact democracy—apparently based on the dictatorship of the masses, but in which the masses have only power enough to insure universal servitude, according to the following prescription borrowed from the old absolutism:
> The indivisibility of power;
> All-absorbing centralism;
> The systematic destruction of all individual, corporate, or local thought believed to be subversive;
> An inquisitorial police force.

[The authoritarian socialists call for a "revolution from above."] They "believe that the State must continue after the Revolution. They preserve the State, power, authority, and government, increasing their scope still further. All they do is to change the titles . . . as though changing the names were enough to transform things!" And Proudhon concludes by saying: "Government is by its nature counter-revolutionary . . . give power to a Saint Vincent de Paul and he will be a Guizot* or a Talleyrand."

Bakunin extended this criticism of authoritarian socialism:

> I detest communism because it is the negation of liberty and I cannot conceive anything human without liberty. I am not a communist because communism concentrates all the powers of society and absorbs them into the State, because it leads inevitably to the centralization of property in the hands of the State, while I want to see the State abolished. I want the complete elimination of the authoritarian principle of state tutelage which has always subjected, oppressed, exploited, and depraved men while claiming to moralize and civilize them. I want society, and collective or social property, to be organized from the bottom up through free association and not from the top down by authority of any kind. . . . In that sense I am a collectivist and not at all a communist.

Soon after making the above speech Bakunin joined the First

---

* Guizot, a minister under Louis Philippe, was known for his extreme conservative views. (Translator's note.)

International. And there he and his supporters came into conflict not only with Marx and Engels but with others far more vulnerable to his attacks than the two founders of scientific socialism: on the one hand, the German social democrats for whom the State was a fetish and who proposed the use of the ballot and electoral alliances to introduce an ambiguous "People's State" (*Volkstaat*); on the other hand, the Blanquists* who sang the virtues of a transitional dictatorship by a revolutionary minority. Bakunin fought these divergent but equally authoritarian concepts tooth and nail, while Marx and Engels oscillated between them for tactical reasons but finally decided to disavow both under the harassment of anarchist criticism.

However, the friction between Bakunin and Marx arose mainly from the sectarian and personal way in which the latter tried to control the International, especially after 1870. There is no doubt that there were wrongs on both sides in this quarrel, in which the stake was the control of the organization and thus of the whole movement of the international working class. Bakunin was not without fault and his case against Marx often lacked fairness and even good faith. What is important for the modern reader, however, is that as early as 1870 Bakunin had the merit of raising the alarm against certain ideas of organization of the working-class movement and of proletarian power which were much later to distort the Russian Revolution. Sometimes unjustly, and sometimes with reason, Bakunin claimed to see in Marxism the embryo of what was to become Leninism and then the malignant growth of Stalinism.

Bakunin maliciously attributed to Marx and Engels ideas which these two men never expressed openly, if indeed they harbored them at all:

> But, it will be said all the workers . . . cannot become scholars; and is it not enough that with this organization [the International] there is a group of men who have mastered the science, philosophy, and politics of socialism as completely as is possible in our day, so that the majority . . . can be certain of remaining on the right

---

* Followers of Auguste Blanqui (1805–1881), French socialist and revolutionary, advocate of insurrection by minorities. (Translator's note.)

road to the final emancipation of the proletariat . . . simply by faithfully obeying their directions? . . . We have heard this line of reasoning developed by innuendo with all sorts of subtle and skillful qualifications but never openly expressed—they are not brave enough or frank enough for that.

Bakunin continued his diatribe:

> Beginning from the basic principle . . . that thought takes precedence over life, and abstract theory over social practice, and inferring that sociological science must become the starting point of social upheaval and reconstruction, they were forced to the conclusion that since thought, theory, and science are, for the present at any rate, the exclusive possessions of a very small number of persons, that minority must direct social life.

The supposed Popular State would be nothing but the despotic government of the popular masses by a new and very narrow aristocracy of knowledge, real or pretended.

Bakunin translated Marx's major work, *Das Kapital*, into Russian, had a lively admiration for his intellectual capacity, fully accepted the materialist conception of history, and appreciated better than anyone Marx's theoretical contribution to the emancipation of the working class. What he would not concede was that intellectual superiority can confer upon anyone the right to lead the working-class movement:

> One asks oneself how a man as intelligent as Marx could conceive of such a heresy against common sense and historical experience as the notion that a group of individuals, however intelligent and well-intentioned, could become the soul and the unifying and directing will of a revolutionary movement and of the economic organization of the proletariat of all countries. . . . The creation of a universal dictatorship . . . , a dictatorship which would somehow perform the task of chief engineer of the world revolution, regulating and steering the insurrectionary movements of the masses of all nations as one steers a machine . . . , the creation of such a dictatorship would in itself suffice to kill the revolution and paralyze and distort all popular movements. . . . And what is one to think of an international congress which, in the supposed interest of this revolution, imposes on the proletariat of the civilized world a government invested with dictatorial powers?

No doubt Bakunin was distorting the thoughts of Marx quite severely in attributing to him such a universally authoritarian concept, but the experience of the Third International has since shown that the danger of which he warned did eventually materialize.

The Russian exile showed himself equally clear-sighted about the danger of state control under a communist regime. According to him, the aspirations of "doctrinaire" socialists would "put the people into a new harness." They doubtless profess, as do the libertarians, to see any State as oppressive, but maintain that only dictatorship—their own, of course—can create freedom for the people; to which the reply is that every dictatorship must seek to last as long as possible. Instead of leaving it to the people to destroy the State, they want to "transfer it . . . into the hands of the benefactors, guardians, and teachers, the leaders of the Communist Party." They see quite well that such a government, "however democratic its forms, will be a real dictatorship," and "console themselves with the idea that it will be temporary and short-lived." But no! Bakunin retorted. This supposedly interim dictatorship will inevitably lead to "the reconstruction of the State, its privileges, its inequalities, and all its oppressions," to the formation of a governmental aristocracy "which again begins to exploit and rule in the name of common happiness or to save the State." And this State will be "the more absolute because its despotism is carefully concealed under obsequious respect . . . for the will of the people."

Bakunin, always particularly lucid, believed in the Russian Revolution: "If the workers of the West wait too long, Russian peasants will set them an example." In Russia, the revolution will be basically "anarchistic." But he was fearful of the outcome: the revolutionaries might well simply carry on the State of Peter the Great which was "based on . . . suspension of all expressions of the life of the people," for "one can change the label of a State and its form . . . but the foundation will remain unchanged." Either the State must be destroyed or one must "reconcile oneself to the vilest and most dangerous lie of our century . . . : *Red Bureaucracy.*" Bakunin summed it up as follows: "Take the most radical of revolutionaries and place him on the throne of all the

Russias or give him dictatorial powers . . . and before the year
is out he will be worse than the Czar himself.")

In Russia Voline was participant, witness, and historian of
the Revolution, and afterward recorded that events had taught
the same lesson as the masters. Yes, indeed, socialist power and
social revolution "are contradictory factors"; they cannot be reconciled:

> A revolution which is inspired by state socialism and adopts this
> form, even "provisionally" and "temporarily," is lost: it takes a
> wrong road down an ever steeper slope. . . . All political power
> inevitably creates a privileged position for those who exercise it. . . .
> Having taken over the Revolution, mastered it, and harnessed it,
> those in power are obliged to create the bureaucratic and repressive
> apparatus which is indispensable for any authority that wants to
> maintain itself, to command, to give orders, in a word: to govern.
> . . . All authority seeks to some extent to control social life. Its
> existence predisposes the masses to passivity, its very presence suffo-
> cates any spirit of initiative. . . . "Communist" power is . . . a
> real bludgeon. Swollen with "authority" . . . it fears every inde-
> pendent action. Any autonomous action is immediately seen as
> suspect, threatening, . . . for such authority wants sole control of
> the tiller. Initiative from any other source is seen as an intrusion
> upon its domain and an infringement of its prerogatives and, there-
> fore, unacceptable.

Further, anarchists categorically deny the need for "provisional"
and "temporary" stages. In 1936, on the eve of the Spanish
Revolution, Diego Abad de Santillan placed authoritarian socialism on the horns of a dilemma: "Either the revolution gives
social wealth to the producers, or it does not. If it does, the producers organize themselves for collective production and distribution and there is nothing left for the State to do. If it does not give
social wealth to the producers, the revolution is nothing but a
deception and the State goes on." One can say that the dilemma is
oversimplified here; it would be less so if it were translated into
terms of intent: the anarchists are not so naïve as to dream that
all the remnants of the State would disappear overnight, but they
have the will to make them wither away as quickly as possible;
while the authoritarians, on the other hand, are satisfied with the

perspective of the indefinite survival of a "temporary" State, arbitrarily termed a "Workers' State."

SOURCES OF INSPIRATION: THE INDIVIDUAL

The anarchist sets two sources of revolutionary energy against the constraints and hierarchies of authoritarian socialism: the individual, and the spontaneity of the masses. Some anarchists are more individualistic than social, some more social than individualistic. However, one cannot conceive of a libertarian who is not an individualist. The observations made by Augustin Hamon from the survey mentioned earlier confirm this analysis.

Max Stirner* rehabilitated the individual at a time when the philosophical field was dominated by Hegelian anti-individualism and most reformers in the social field had been led by the misdeeds of bourgeois egotism to stress its opposite: was not the very word "socialism" created as antonym to "individualism"?

Stirner exalted the intrinsic value of the unique individual, that is to say, one cast in a single unrepeatable mold (an idea which has been confirmed by recent biological research). For a long time this thinker remained isolated in anarchist circles, an eccentric followed by only a tiny sect of intelligent individualists. Today, the boldness and scope of his thought appear in a new light. The contemporary world seems to have set itself the task of rescuing the individual from all the forms of alienation which crush him, those of individual slavery and those of totalitarian conformism. In a famous article written in 1933, Simone Weil complained of not finding in Marxist writings any answer to questions arising from the need to defend the individual against the new forms of oppression coming after classical capitalist oppression. Stirner set out to fill this serious gap as early as the mid-nineteenth century.

He wrote in a lively style, crackling with aphorisms: "Do not

* In his book *The Ego and His Own.*

seek in self-renunciation a freedom which denies your very selves, but seek your own selves. . . . Let each of you be an all-powerful I."[There is no freedom but that which the individual conquers for himself.] Freedom given or conceded is not freedom but "stolen goods." "There is no judge but myself who can decide whether I am right or wrong." "The only things I have no right to do are those I do not do with a free mind." "You have the right to be whatever you have the strength to be." Whatever you accomplish you accomplish as a unique individual: "Neither the State, society, nor humanity can master this devil."

In order to emancipate himself, the individual must begin by putting under the microscope the intellectual baggage with which his parents and teachers have saddled him. He must undertake a vast operation of "desanctification," beginning with the so-called morality of the bourgeoisie: "Like the bourgeoisie itself, its native soil, it is still far too close to the heaven of religion, is still not free enough, and uncritically borrows bourgeois laws to transplant them to its own ground instead of working out new and independent doctrines."

Stirner was especially incensed by sexual morality. The "machinations" of Christianity "against passion" have simply been taken over by the secularists. They refused to listen to the appeal of the flesh and display their zeal against it. They "spit in the face of immorality." The moral prejudices inculcated by Christianity have an especially strong hold on the masses of the people. "The people furiously urge the police on against anything which seems to them immoral or even improper, and this public passion for morality protects the police as an institution far more effectively than a government could ever do."

Stirner foreshadowed modern psychoanalysis by observing and denouncing the internalization of parental moral values. From childhood we are consumed with moral prejudices. Morality has become "an internal force from which I cannot free myself," "its despotism is ten times worse than before, because it now scolds away from within my conscience." "The young are sent to school in herds to learn the old saws and when they know the verbiage of the old by heart they are said to have come of age." Stirner declared himself an iconoclast: "God, conscience, duties, and laws are all errors which have been stuffed into our minds and hearts." The real seducers and corrupters of youth are the priests and parents who "muddy young hearts and stupefy young minds." If there is anything that "comes from the devil" it is surely this false divine voice which has been interpolated into the conscience.

In the process of rehabilitating the individual, Stirner also discovered the Freudian subconscious. The Self cannot be apprehended. Against it "the empire of thought, mind, and ratiocination crumbles"; it is inexpressible, inconceivable, incomprehensible, and through Stirner's lively aphorisms one seems to hear the first echoes of existentialist philosophy: "I start from a hypothesis by taking myself as hypothesis. . . . I use it solely for my enjoyment and satisfaction. . . . I exist only because I nourish my Self. . . . The fact that I am of absorbing interest to myself means that I exist."

Of course the white heat of imagination in which Stirner wrote sometimes misled him into paradoxical statements. He let slip some antisocial aphorisms and arrived at the position that life in society is impossible: "We do not aspire to communal life but to a life apart." "The people is dead! Good-day, Self!" "The people's good fortune is my misfortune!" "If it is right for *me*, it is right. It is possible that it is wrong for others: let them take care of themselves!"

However, these occasional outbursts are probably not a fundamental part of his thinking and, in spite of his hermit's bluster, he aspired to communal life. Like most people who are introverted, isolated, shut in, he suffered acute nostalgia for it. To those who asked how he could live in society with his exclusiveness he replied that only the man who has comprehended his own "oneness" can have relations with his fellows. The individual needs help and friends; for example, if he writes books he needs readers. He joins with his fellow man in order to increase his strength and fulfill himself more completely through their combined strength than either could in isolation. "If you have several million others behind you to protect you, together you will become a great force and will easily be victorious"—but on one condition: these relations with others must be free and voluntary and always subject to repudiation. Stirner distinguishes a society already established, which is a constraint, from association, which is a voluntary act. ["Society uses *you*, but you use association."] Admittedly, association implies a sacrifice, a restriction upon freedom, but this sacrifice is not made for the common good: "It is my own personal interest that brings me to it."

Stirner was dealing with very contemporary problems, especially when he treated the question of political parties with special reference to the communists. He was severely critical of the conformism of parties: "One must follow one's party everywhere and anywhere, absolutely approving and defending its basic principles." "Members . . . bow to the slightest wishes of the party." The party's program must "be for them certain, above question. . . . One must belong to the party body and soul. . . . Anyone who goes from one party to another is immediately treated as a renegade." In Stirner's view, a monolithic party ceases to be an association and only a corpse remains. He rejected such a party but did not give up hope of joining a political association: "I shall always find enough people who want to associate with me without having to swear allegiance to my flag." He felt he could only rejoin the party if there was "nothing compulsory about it," and his sole condition was that he could be sure "of not letting himself be taken over by the party." "The party is nothing other than a party in which he takes part." "He associates freely and takes back his freedom in the same way."

There is only one weakness in Stirner's argument, though it more or less underlies all his writings: his concept of the unity of the individual is not only "egotistical," profitable for the "Self" but is also valid for the collectivity. The human association is only fruitful if it does not crush the individual but, on the contrary, develops initiative and creative energy. Is not the strength of a party the sum of all the strengths of the individuals who compose it? This lacuna in his argument is due to the fact that Stirner's synthesis of the individual and society remained halting and incomplete. In the thought of this rebel the social and the antisocial clash and are not always resolved. The social anarchists were to reproach him for this, quite rightly.

These reproaches were the more bitter because Stirner, presumably through ignorance, made the mistake of including Proudhon among the authoritarian communists who condemn individualist aspirations in the name of "social duty." It is true that Proudhon had mocked Stirner-like "adoration" of the individual,* but his entire work was a search for a synthesis, or rather an "equilibrium" between concern for the individual and the interests of society, between individual power and collective power. "Just as individualism is a primordial human trait, so association is its complement."

> Some think that man has value only through society . . . and tend to absorb the individual into the collectivity. Thus . . . the communist system is a devaluation of the personality in the name of society. . . . That is tyranny, a mystical and anonymous tyranny, it is not association. . . . When the human personality is divested of its prerogatives, society is found to be without its vital principle.

On the other hand, Proudhon rejected the individualistic utopianism that agglomerates unrelated individualities with no organic connection, no collective power, and thus betrays its inability to resolve the problem of common interests. In conclusion: neither communism nor unlimited freedom. "We have too many joint interests, too many things in common."

Bakunin, also, was both an individualist and a socialist. He kept reiterating that a society could only reach a higher level by starting from the free individual. Whenever he enunciated rights which must be guaranteed to groups, such as the right to self-determination or secession, he was careful to state that the individual should be the first to benefit from them. The individual owes duties to society only in so far as he has freely consented to become part of it. Everyone is free to associate or not to associate, and, if he so desires, "to go and live in the deserts or the forests among the wild beasts." "Freedom is the absolute right of every human being to seek no other sanction for his actions but his own conscience, to determine these actions solely by his own will, and consequently to owe his first responsibility to himself alone." The society which the individual has freely chosen to join as a member appears only as a secondary factor in the above list of responsibil-

---

* Without direct mention of Stirner, whose work he may not, therefore, have read.

ities. It has more duties to the individual than rights over him, and, provided he has reached his majority, should exercise "neither surveillance nor authority" over him, but owe him "the protection of his liberty."

Bakunin pushed the practice of "absolute and complete liberty" very far: I am entitled to dispose of my person as I please, to be idle or active, to live either honestly by my own labor or even by shamefully exploiting charity or private confidence. All this on one condition only: that this charity or confidence is voluntary and given to me only by individuals who have attained their majority. I even have the right to enter into associations whose objects make them "immoral" or apparently so. In his concern for liberty Bakunin went so far as to allow one to join associations designed to corrupt and destroy individual or public liberty: ["Liberty can and must defend itself only through liberty] to try to restrict it on the specious pretext of defending it is a dangerous contradiction."

As for ethical problems, Bakunin was sure "immorality" was a consequence of a viciously organized society. This latter must, therefore, be destroyed from top to bottom. Liberty alone can bring moral improvement. Restrictions imposed on the pretext of improving morals have always proved detrimental to them. Far from checking the spread of immorality, repression has always extended and deepened it. Thus it is futile to oppose it by rigorous legislation which trespasses on individual liberty. Bakunin allowed only one sanction against the idle, parasitic, or wicked: the loss of political rights, that is, of the safeguards accorded the individual by society. It follows that each individual has the right to alienate his own freedom by his own acts but, in this case, is denied the enjoyment of his political rights for the duration of his voluntary servitude.

If crimes are committed they must be seen as a disease, and punishment as treatment rather than as social vengeance. Moreover, the convicted individual must retain the right not to submit to the sentence imposed if he declares that he no longer wishes to be a member of the society concerned. The latter, in return, has the right to expel such an individual and declare him to be outside its protection.

Bakunin, however, was far from being a nihilist. His proclamation of absolute individual freedom did not lead him to repudiate all social obligations. I become free only through the freedom of others: ["Man can fulfill his free individuality only by complementing it through all the individuals around him, and only through work and the collective force of society."] Membership in the society is voluntary but Bakunin had no doubt that because of its enormous advantages "membership will be chosen by all." Man is both "the most individual and the most social of the animals."

Bakunin showed no softness for egoism in its vulgar sense—for bourgeois individualism "which drives the individual to conquest and the establishment of his own well-being . . . in spite of everyone, on the backs of others, to their detriment." "Such a solitary and abstract human being is as much a fiction as God." "Total isolation is intellectual, moral, and material death."

A broad and synthesizing intellect, Bakunin attempts to create a bridge between individuals and mass movements: "All social life is simply this continual mutual dependence of individuals and the masses. Even the strongest and most intelligent individuals . . . are at every moment of their lives both promoters and products of the desires and actions of the masses." The anarchist sees the revolutionary movement as the product of this interaction; thus he regards individual action and autonomous collective action by the masses as equally fruitful and militant.

The Spanish anarchists were the intellectual heirs of Bakunin. Although enamored of socialization, on the very eve of the 1936 Revolution they did not fail to make a solemn pledge to protect the sacred autonomy of the individual: "The eternal aspiration to be unique," wrote Diego Abad de Santillan, "will be expressed in a thousand ways: the individual will not be suffocated by leveling down . . . . Individualism, personal taste, and originality will have adequate scope to express themseves."

SOURCES OF INSPIRATION:
THE MASSES

From the Revolution of 1848 Proudhon learned that the masses
are the source of power of revolutions. At the end of 1849 he
wrote: "Revolutions have no instigators; they come when fate
beckons, and end with the exhaustion of the mysterious power
that makes them flourish." "All revolutions have been carried
through by the spontaneous action of the people; if occasionally
governments have responded to the initiative of the people it was
only because they were forced or constrained to do so. Almost
always they blocked, repressed, struck." "When left to their own
instincts the people almost always see better than when guided
by the policy of leaders." "A social revolution . . . does not occur
at the behest of a master with a ready-made theory, or at the dictate of a prophet. A truly organic revolution is a product of universal life, and although it has its messengers and executors it is
really not the work of any one person." The revolution must be
conducted from below and not from above. Once the revolutionary
crisis is over social reconstruction should be the task of the popular masses themselves. Proudhon affirmed the "personality and
autonomy of the masses."

Bakunin also repeated tirelessly that a social revolution can be
neither decreed nor organized from above and can only be made
and fully developed by spontaneous and continuous mass action.
Revolutions come "like a thief in the night." They are "produced
by the force of events." "They are long in preparation in the
depths of the instinctive consciousness of the masses—then they
explode, often precipitated by apparently trivial causes." "One
can foresee them, have presentiments of their approach . . . ,
but one can never accelerate their outbreak." "The anarchist social revolution . . . arises spontaneously in the hearts of the
people, destroying all that hinders the generous upsurge of the life
of the people in order thereafter to create new forms of free social
life which will arise from the very depths of the soul of the

people." Bakunin saw in the Commune of 1871 striking confirmation of his views. The Communards believed that "the action of individuals was almost nothing" in the social revolution and the "spontaneous action of the masses should be everything."

Like his predecessors, Kropotkin praised "this admirable sense of spontaneous organization which the people . . . has in such a high degree, but is so rarely permitted to apply." He added, playfully, that "only he who has always lived with his nose buried in official papers and red tape could doubt it."

Having made all these generous and optimistic affirmations, both the anarchist and his brother and enemy the Marxist confront a grave contradiction. The spontaneity of the masses is essential, an absolute priority, but not sufficient in itself. The assistance of a revolutionary minority capable of thinking out the revolution has proved to be necessary to raise mass consciousness. How is this élite to be prevented from exploiting its intellectual superiority to usurp the role of the masses, paralyze their initiative, and even impose a new domination upon them?

After his idyllic exaltation of spontaneity, Proudhon came to admit the inertia of the masses, to deplore the prejudice in favor of governments, the deferential instinct and the inferiority complex which inhibit an upsurge of the people. [Thus the collective action of the people must be stimulated, and if no revelation were to come to them from outside, the servitude of the lower classes might go on indefinitely.] And he admitted that "in every epoch the ideas which stirred the masses had first been germinated in the minds of a few thinkers. . . . The multitude never took the initiative. . . . Individuality has priority in every movement of the human spirit." It would be ideal if these conscious minorities were to pass on to the people their science, the science of revolution. But in practice Proudhon seemed to be skeptical about such a synthesis: to expect it would be to underestimate the intrusive nature of authority. At best, it might be possible to "balance" the two elements.

Before his conversion to anarchism in 1864, Bakunin was involved in conspiracies and secret societies and became familiar with the typically Blanquist idea that minority action must precede the awakening of the broad masses and combine with their

most advanced elements after dragging them out of their lethargy.
The problem appeared different in the workers' International, when
that vast movement was at last established. Although he had
become an anarchist, Bakunin remained convinced of the need
for a conscious vanguard: "For revolution to triumph over reaction the unity of revolutionary thought and action must have an
organ in the midst of the popular anarchy which will be the
very life and the source of all the energy of the revolution." A
group, small or large, of individuals inspired by the same idea,
and sharing a common purpose, will produce "a natural effect
on the masses." "Ten, twenty, or thirty men with a clear understanding and good organization, knowing what they want and
where they are going, can easily carry with them a hundred, two
hundred, three hundred or even more." "We must create the
well-organized and rightly inspired general staffs of the leaders
of the mass movement."

The methods advocated by Bakunin are very similar to what is
nowadays termed "infiltration." It consists of working clandestinely
upon the most intelligent and influential individuals in each locality "so that [each] organization should conform to our ideas
as far as possible. That is the whole secret of our influence." The
anarchists must be like "invisible pilots" in the midst of the
stormy masses. They must direct them not by "ostensible power,"
but by "a dictatorship without insignia, title, or official rights,
all the more powerful because it will have none of the marks of
power." Bakunin was quite aware how little his terminology
("leaders," "dictatorship," etc.) differed from that of the opponents of anarchism, and replied in advance "to anyone who alleges
that action organized in this way is yet another assault upon the
liberty of the masses, an attempt to create a new authoritarian
power": No! the vanguard must be neither the benefactor nor the
dictatorial leader of the people but simply the midwife to its
self-liberation. It can achieve nothing more than to spread among
the masses ideas which correspond with their instincts. The rest
can and must be done by the people themselves. The "revolutionary authorities" (Bakunin did not draw back from using this
term but excused it by expressing the hope that they would be
"as few as possible") were not to impose the revolution on the

masses but arouse it in their midst; were not to subject them to
any form of organization, but stimulate their autonomous organization from below to the top.

Much later, Rosa Luxemburg was to elucidate what Bakunin
had surmised: that the contradiction between libertarian spontaneity and the need for action by conscious vanguards would only
be fully resolved when science and the working class became fused,
and the masses became fully conscious, needing no more "leaders,"
but only "executive organs" of their "conscious action." After
emphasizing that the proletariat still lacked science and organization, the Russian anarchist reached the conclusion that the International could only become an instrument of emancipation
"when it had caused the science, philosophy, and politics of
socialism to penetrate the reflective consciousness of each of its
members."

However theoretically satisfying this synthesis might be, it was
a draft drawn on a very distant future. Until historical evolution
made it possible to accomplish it, the anarchists remained, like the
Marxists, more or less imprisoned by contradiction. It was to rend
the Russian Revolution, torn between the spontaneous power of
the soviets and the claim of the Bolshevik Party to a "directing
role." It was to show itself in the Spanish Revolution, where the
libertarians were to swing from one extreme to the other, from
the mass movement to the conscious anarchist élite.

Two historical examples will suffice to illustrate this contradiction.

The anarchists were to draw one categorical conclusion from
the experience of the Russian Revolution: a condemnation of
the "leading role" of the Party. Voline formulated it in this way:

> The key idea of anarchism is simple: no party, or political or
> ideological group, even if it sincerely desires to do so, will ever
> succeed in emancipating the working masses by placing itself above
> or outside them in order to "govern" or "guide" them. True eman-
> cipation can only be brought about by the direct action . . . of
> those concerned, the workers themselves, through their own class
> organizations (production syndicates, factory committees, coopera-
> tives, etc.) and not under the banner of any political party or
> ideological body. Their emancipation must be based on concrete

action and "self-administration," aided but not controlled by revolutionaries working from within the masses and not from above them. . . . The anarchist idea and the true emancipatory revolution can never be brought to fruition by anarchists as such but only by the vast masses . . . , anarchists, or other revolutionaries in general, are required only to enlighten or aid them in certain situations. ⌈If anarchists maintained that they could bring about a social revolution by "guiding" the masses, such a pretension would be as illusory as that of the Bolsheviks and for the same reasons.⌉

However, the Spanish anarchists, in their turn, were to experience the need to organize an ideologically conscious minority, the Iberian Anarchist Federation (FAI), within their vast trade-union organization, the National Confederation of Labor (CNT). This was to combat the reformist tendencies of some "pure" syndicalists and the maneuvers of the agents of the "dictatorship of the proletariat." The FAI drew its inspiration from the ideas of Bakunin, and so tried to enlighten rather than to direct. The relatively high libertarian consciousness of many of the rank-and-file members of the CNT also helped it to avoid the excesses of the authoritarian revolutionary parties. It did not, however, perform its part as guide very well, being clumsy and hesitant about its tutelage over the trade unions, irresolute in its strategy, and more richly endowed with activists and demagogues than with revolutionaries as clear-thinking on the level of theory as on that of practice.

Relations between the masses and the conscious minority constitute a problem to which no full solution has been found by the Marxists or even by the anarchists, and one on which it seems that the last word has not yet been said.

2

In Search of a New Society

ANARCHISM IS NOT UTOPIAN

Because anarchism is constructive, anarchist theory emphatically rejects the charge of utopianism. It uses the historical method in an attempt to prove that the society of the future is not an anarchist invention, but the actual product of the hidden effects of past events. Proudhon affirmed that for 6,000 years humanity had been crushed by an inexorable system of authority but had been sustained by a "secret virtue": "Beneath the apparatus of government, under the shadow of its political institutions, society was slowly and silently producing its own organization, making for itself a new order which expressed its vitality and autonomy."

[However harmful government may have been, it contained its own negation] It was always "a phenomenon of collective life, the public exercise of the powers of our law, an expression of social spontaneity, all serving to prepare humanity for a higher state. What humanity seeks in religion and calls 'God' is itself. What the citizen seeks in government . . . is likewise himself— it is liberty." The French Revolution hastened this inexorable advance toward anarchy: "The day that our fathers . . . stated the principle of the free exercise of all his faculties by man as a citizen, on that day authority was repudiated in heaven and on earth, and government, even by delegation, became impossible."

The Industrial Revolution did the rest. From then on politics was overtaken by the economy and subordinated to it. Government could no longer escape the direct competition of producers and became in reality no more than the relation between different interests. This revolution was completed by the growth of the proletariat. In spite of its protestations, authority now expressed only socialism: "The Napoleonic code is as useless to the new

41

society as the Platonic republic: within a few years the absolute law of property will have everywhere been replaced by the relative and mobile law of industrial cooperation, and it will then be necessary to reconstruct this cardboard castle from top to bottom."

Bakunin, in turn, recognized "the immense and undeniable service rendered to humanity by the French Revolution which is father to us all." The principle of authority has been eliminated from the people's consciousness forever and order imposed from above has henceforth become impossible. All that remains is to "organize society so that it can live without government." Bakunin relied on popular tradition to achieve this. ["In spite of the oppressive and harmful tutelage of the State," the masses have, through the centuries, "spontaneously developed within themselves many, if not all, of the essential elements of the material and moral order of real human unity."]

THE NEED FOR ORGANIZATION

Anarchist theory does not see itself as a synonym for disorganization. Proudhon was the first to proclaim that anarchism is not disorder but order, is the natural order in contrast to the artificial order imposed from above, is true unity as against the false unity brought about by constraint. Such a society "thinks, speaks, and acts like a man, precisely because it is no longer represented by a man, no longer recognizes personal authorities; because, like every organized living being, like the infinite of Pascal, it has its center everywhere and its circumference nowhere." Anarchy is "organized, living society," "the highest degree of liberty and order to which humanity can aspire." Perhaps some anarchists thought otherwise but the Italian Errico Malatesta called them to order:

> Under the influence of the authoritarian education given to them, they think that authority is the soul of social organization and repudiate the latter in order to combat the former . . . . Those anarchists opposed to organization make the fundamental error of believing that organization is impossible without authority. Having accepted this hypothesis they reject any kind of organization rather

than accept the minimum of authority . . . . If we believed that organization could not exist without authority we would be authoritarians, because we would still prefer the authority which imprisons and saddens life to the disorganization which makes it impossible.

The twentieth-century anarchist Voline developed and clarified this idea:

A mistaken—or, more often, deliberately inaccurate—interpretation alleges that the libertarian concept means the absence of all organization. This is entirely false: it is not a matter of "organization" or "nonorganization," but of two different principles of organization . . . . Of course, say the anarchists, society must be organized. However, the new organization . . . must be established freely, socially, and, above all, from below. The principle of organization must not issue from a center created in advance to capture the whole and impose itself upon it but, on the contrary, it must come from all sides to create nodes of coordination, natural centers to serve all these points . . . . On the other hand, the other kind of "organization," copied from that of the old oppressive and exploitative society, . . . would exaggerate all the blemishes of the old society . . . . It could then only be maintained by means of a new artifice.

In effect, the anarchists would be not only protagonists of true organization but "first-class organizers," as Henri Lefebvre admitted in his book on the Commune. But this philosopher thought he saw a contradiction here—"a rather surprising contradiction which we find repeatedly in the history of the working-class movement up to present times, especially in Spain." It can only "astonish" those for whom libertarians are *a priori* disorganizers.

SELF-MANAGEMENT

When Marx and Engels drafted the Communist Manifesto of 1848, on the eve of the February Revolution, they foresaw, at any rate for a long transitional period, all the means of production centralized in the hands of an all-embracing State. They took

over Louis Blanc's authoritarian idea of conscripting both agricultural and industrial workers into "armies of labor." Proudhon was the first to propound an anti-statist form of economic
management.

During the February Revolution workers' associations for production sprang up spontaneously in Paris and in Lyon. In 1848
this beginning of self-management seemed to Proudhon far more
the revolutionary event than did the political revolution. It had
not been invented by a theoretician or preached by doctrinaires,
it was not the State which provided the original stimulus; but the
people. Proudhon urged the workers to organize in this way in
every part of the Republic, to draw in small property, trade, and
industry, then large property and establishments, and, finally, the
greatest enterprises of all (mines, canals, railways, etc.), and
thus "become masters of all."

The present tendency is to remember only Proudhon's naïve
and passing idea of preserving small-scale trade and artisans' workshops. This was certainly naïve, and doubtless uneconomic, but
his thinking on this point was ambivalent. Proudhon was a living
contradiction: he castigated property as a source of injustice and
exploitation and had a weakness for it, although only to the extent that he saw in it a guarantee of the independence of the
individual. Moreover, Proudhon is too often confused with what
Bakunin called "the little so-called Proudhonian coterie" which
gathered around him in his last years. This rather reactionary group
was stillborn. In the First International it tried in vain to put
across private ownership of the means of production against collectivism. The chief reason this group was short-lived was that
most of its adherents were all too easily convinced by Bakunin's
arguments and abandoned their so-called Proudhonian ideas to
support collectivism.

In the last analysis, this group, who called themselves *mutuel-
listes*, were only partly opposed to collectivism: they rejected it for
agriculture because of the individualism of the French peasant,
but accepted it for transport, and in matters of industrial self-
management actually demanded it while rejecting its name. Their
fear of the word was largely due to their uneasiness in the face
of the temporary united front set up against them by Bakunin's

collectivist disciples and certain authoritarian Marxists who were almost open supporters of state control of the economy.

Proudhon really moved with the times and realized that it is impossible to turn back the clock. He was realistic enough to understand that "small industry is as stupid as petty culture" and recorded this view in his *Carnets*. With regard to large-scale modern industry requiring a large labor force, he was resolutely collectivist: "In future, large-scale industry and wide culture must be the fruit of association." "We have no choice in the matter," he concluded, and waxed indignant that anyone had dared to suggest that he was opposed to technical progress.

In his collectivism he was, however, as categorically opposed to statism. Property must be abolished. The community (as it is understood by authoritarian communism) is oppression and servitude. Thus Proudhon sought a combination of property and community: this was association. The means of production and exchange must be controlled neither by capitalist companies nor by the State. Since they are to the men who work in them "what the hive is to the bee," they must be managed by associations of workers, and only thus will collective powers cease to be "alienated" for the benefit of a few exploiters. "We, the workers, associated or about to be associated," wrote Proudhon in the style of a manifesto,

> do not need the State . . . . Exploitation by the State always means rulers and wage slaves. We want the government of man by man no more than the exploitation of man by man. Socialism is the opposite of governmentalism . . . . We want these associations to be . . . the first components of a vast federation of associations and groups united in the common bond of the democratic and social republic.

Proudhon went into detail and enumerated precisely the essential features of workers' self-management:

—Every associated individual to have an indivisible share in the property of the company.

—Each worker to take his share of the heavy and repugnant tasks.

—Each to go through the gamut of operations and instruction,

of grades and activities, to insure that he has the widest training.
Proudhon was insistent on the point that "the worker must go
through all the operations of the industry he is attached to."

—Office-holders to be elected and regulations submitted to the
associates for approval.

—Remuneration to be proportionate to the nature of the position held, the degree of skill, and the responsibility carried. Every
associate to share in the profits in proportion to the service he has
given.

—Each to be free to set his own hours, carry on his duties, and
to leave the association at will.

—The associated workers to choose their leaders, engineers, ar-
chitects, and accountants. Proudhon stressed the fact that the
proletariat still lacks technicians: hence the need to bring into
workers' self-management programs "industrial and commercial
persons of distinction" who would teach the workers business
methods and receive fixed salaries in return: there is "room for all
in the sunshine of the revolution."

This libertarian concept of self-management is at the opposite
pole from the paternalistic, statist form of self-management set
out by Louis Blanc in a draft law of September 15, 1849. The
author of *The Organization of Labor* wanted to create workers'
associations sponsored and financed by the State. He proposed
an arbitrary division of the profits as follows: 25 percent to a
capital amortization fund; 25 percent to a social security fund;
25 percent to a reserve fund; 25 percent to be divided among the
workers.*

Proudhon would have none of self-management of this kind.
In his view the associated workers must not "submit to the State,"
but "be the State itself." "Association . . . can do everything
and reform everything without interference from authority, can
encroach upon authority and subjugate it." Proudhon wanted "to

---

* Cf. the 1963 decrees by which the Algerian Republic institutionalized
the self-management which had been originated spontaneously by the peasants. The apportionment—if not the actual percentages—is very similar, and
the last quarter, "to be divided among the workers," is the same as the
"balance" over which there was controversy in Algeria.

go toward government through association, not to association through government." He issued a warning against the illusion, cherished in the dreams of authoritarian socialists, that the State could tolerate free self-management. How could it endure "the formation of enemy enclaves alongside a centralized authority"? Proudhon prophetically warned: "While centralization continues to endow the State with colossal force, nothing can be achieved by spontaneous initiative or by the independent actions of groups and individuals."

It should be stressed that in the congresses of the First International the libertarian idea of self-management prevailed over the statist concept. At the Lausanne Congress in 1867 the committee reporter, a Belgian called César de Paepe, proposed that the State should become the owner of undertakings that were to be nationalized. At that time Charles Longuet was a libertarian, and he replied: "All right, on condition that it is understood that we define the State as 'the collective of the citizens' . . . , also that these services will be administered not by state functionaries . . . but by groupings of workers." The debate continued the following year (1868) at the Brussels Congress and this time the same committee reporter took care to be precise on this point: "Collective property would belong to society as a whole, but would be conceded to associations of workers. The State would be no more than a federation of various groups of workers." Thus clarified, the resolution was passed.

However, the optimism which Proudhon had expressed in 1848 with regard to self-management was to prove unjustified. Not many years later, in 1857, he severely criticized the existing workers' associations; inspired by naïve, utopian illusions, they had paid the price of their lack of experience. They had become narrow and exclusive, had functioned as collective employers, and had been carried away by hierarchical and managerial concepts. All the abuses of capitalist companies "were exaggerated further in these so-called brotherhoods." They had been torn by discord, rivalry, defections, and betrayals. Once their managers had learned the business concerned, they retired to "set up as bourgeois employers on their own account." In other instances, the members had insisted on dividing up the resources. In 1848 several hundred workers' associations had been set up; nine years later only twenty remained.

As opposed to this narrow and particularist attitude, Proudhon advocated a "universal" and "synthetic" concept of self-management. The task of the future was far more than just "getting a few hundred workers into associations"; it was "the economic transformation of a nation of thirty-six million souls." The workers' associations of the future should work for all and not "operate for the benefit of a few." Self-management, therefore, required the members to have some education: "A man is not born a member of an association, he becomes one." The hardest task before the association is to "educate the members." It is more important to create a "fund of men" than to form a "mass of capital."

With regard to the legal aspect, it had been Proudhon's first idea to vest the ownership of their undertaking in the workers' associations but now he rejected this narrow solution. In order to do this he distinguished between possession and ownership. Ownership is absolute, aristocratic, feudal; possession is democratic, republican, egalitarian: it consists of the enjoyment of an usufruct which can neither be alienated, nor given away, nor sold. The workers should hold their means of production in *alleu* like the ancient Germains,* but would not be the outright owners. Property would be replaced by federal, cooperative ownership vested not in the State but in the producers as a whole, united in a vast agricultural and industrial federation.

Proudhon waxed enthusiastic about the future of such a revised and corrected form of self-management: "It is not false rhetoric that states this, it is an economic and social necessity: the time is near when we shall be unable to progress on any but these new conditions . . . . Social classes . . . must merge into one single producers' association." Would self-management succeed? "On the reply to this . . . depends the whole future of the workers. If it is affirmative an entire new world will open up for humanity; if

---

* *Alleu* is a feudal term for heritable inalienable property. The Germains were a German tribe in which individual freedom was highly developed. (Translator's note.)

it is negative the proletarian can take it as settled . . . . There is no hope for him in this wicked world."

THE BASES OF EXCHANGE

How were dealings between the different workers' associations to be organized? At first Proudhon maintained that the exchange value of all goods could be measured by the amount of labor necessary to produce them. The workers were to be paid in "work vouchers"; trading agencies or social shops were to be set up where they would buy goods at retail prices calculated in hours of work. Large-scale trade would be carried on through a compensatory clearinghouse or People's Bank which would accept payment in work vouchers. This bank would also serve as a credit establishment lending to workers' associations the sums needed for effective operation. The loans would be interest free.

This so-called *mutuelliste* scheme was rather utopian and certainly difficult to operate in a capitalist system. Early in 1849 Proudhon set up the People's Bank and in six weeks some 20,000 people joined, but it was short-lived. It was certainly farfetched to believe that *mutuellisme* would spread like a patch of oil and to exclaim, as Proudhon did then: "It really is the new world, the promised society which is being grafted on to the old and gradually transforming it!"

The idea of wages based on the number of hours worked is debatable on many grounds. The libertarian communists of the Kropotkin school—Malatesta, Elisée Reclus, Carlo Cafiero—did not fail to criticize it. In the first place, they thought it unjust. Cafiero argued that "three hours of Peter's work may be worth five of Paul's." Other factors than duration must be considered in determining the value of labor: intensity, professional and intellectual training, etc. The family commitments of the workers must also be taken into account.* Moreover, in a collectivist regime the worker remains a wage slave of the community that

---

* Cf. a similar discussion in the *Critique of the Gotha Programme*, drafted by Karl Marx in 1875 though not published until 1891.

buys and supervises his labor. Payment by hours of work performed cannot be an ideal solution; at best it would be a temporary expedient. We must put an end to the morality of account books, to the philosophy of "credit and debit." This method of remuneration, derived from modified individualism, is in contradiction to collective ownership of the means of production, and cannot bring about a profound revolutionary change in man. It is incompatible with anarchism; a new form of ownership requires a new form of remuneration. Service to the community cannot be measured in units of money. Needs will have to be given precedence over services, and all the products of the labor of all must belong to all, each to take his share of them freely. *To each according to his need* should be the motto of libertarian communism.

Kropotkin, Malatesta, and their followers seem to have overlooked the fact that Proudhon had anticipated their objections and revised his earlier ideas. In his *Théorie de la Propriété*, published after his death, he explained that he had only supported the idea of equal pay for equal work in his "First Memorandum on Property" of 1840: "I had forgotten to say two things: first, that labor is measured by combining its duration with its intensity; second, that one must not include in the worker's wages the amortization of the cost of his education and the work he did on his own account as an unpaid apprentice, nor the premiums to insure him against the risks he runs, all of which vary in different occupations." Proudhon claimed to have "repaired" this "omission" in his later writings in which he proposed that mutual insurance cooperative associations should compensate for unequal costs and risks. Furthermore, Proudhon did not regard the remuneration of the members of a workers' association as "wages" but as a share of profits freely determined by associated and equally responsible workers. In an as yet unpublished thesis, Pierre Haubtman, one of Proudhon's most recent exponents, comments that workers' self-management would have no meaning if it were not interpreted in this way.

The libertarian communists saw fit to criticize Proudhon's *mutuellisme* and the more logical collectivism of Bakunin for not having determined the way in which labor would be remunerated in a socialist system. These critics seemed to have overlooked the fact that the two founders of anarchism were anxious not to lay down a rigid pattern of society prematurely. They wanted to leave the self-management associations the widest choice in this matter. The libertarian communists themselves were to provide the justification for this flexibility and refusal to jump to conclusions, so different from their own impatient forecasts: they stressed that in the ideal system of their choice "labor would produce more than enough for all" and that "bourgeois" norms of remuneration could only be replaced by specifically "communist" norms when the era of abundance had set in, and not before. In 1884 Malatesta, drafting the program for a projected anarchist international, admitted that communism could be brought about immediately only in a very limited number of areas and, "for the rest," collectivism would have to be accepted "for a transitional period."

> For communism to be possible, a high stage of moral development is required of the members of society, a sense of solidarity both elevated and profound, which the upsurge of the revolution may not suffice to induce. This doubt is the more justified in that material conditions favorable to this development will not exist at the beginning.

Anarchism was about to face the test of experience, on the eve of the Spanish Revolution of 1936, when Diego Abad de Santillan demonstrated the immediate impracticability of libertarian communism in very similar terms. He held that the capitalist system had not prepared human beings for communism: far from developing their social instincts and sense of solidarity it tends in every way to suppress and penalize such feelings.

Santillan recalled the experience of the Russian and other revolutions to persuade the anarchists to be more realistic. He charged them with receiving the most recent lessons of experience with suspicion or superiority. He maintained that it is doubtful whether a revolution would lead directly to the realization of our ideal of communist anarchism. The collectivist watchword, "to each the product of his labor," would be more appropriate than communism to the requirements of the real situation in the first phase of a revolution, when the economy would be disorganized, production at a low ebb, and food supplies a priority. The economic models to be tried would, at best, evolve slowly toward communism. To put human beings brutally behind bars by imprisoning them in rigid forms of social life would be an authoritarian approach which would hinder the revolution. *Mutuellisme,* communism, collectivism are only different means to the same end. Santillan turned back to the wise empiricism of Proudhon and Bakunin, claiming for the coming Spanish Revolution the right to experiment freely: "The degree of *mutuellisme,* collectivism, or communism which can be achieved will be determined freely in each locality and each social sphere." In fact, as will be seen later, the experience of the Spanish "collectives" of 1936 illustrated the difficulties arising from the premature implementation of integral communism.*

COMPETITION

Competition is one of the norms inherited from the bourgeois economy which raises thorny problems when preserved in a collectivist or self-management economy. Proudhon saw it as an "expression of social spontaneity" and the guarantee of the "freedom" of the association. Moreover, it would for a long time to come provide an "irreplaceable stimulus" without which an "immense slackening off" would follow the high tension of industry. He went into detail: "The working brotherhood is pledged to supply society with the goods and services asked from it at prices as near as possible to the cost of production . . . . Thus the workers' association denies itself any amalgamation [of a monopolistic type], subjects itself to the law of competition, and keeps its books and records open to society, which reserves the power to dissolve the association as the ultimate sanction of society's right of supervision." "Competition and association are interdependent . . . . The most deplorable error of socialism is to have considered it [competition] as the disorder of society. There can . . .

---

* Cuba is today gropingly and prematurely trying to find the way to integral communism.

be . . . no question of destroying competition . . . . It is a matter of finding an equilibrium, one could say a policing agent."

Proudhon's attachment to the principle of competition drew the sarcasm of Louis Blanc: "We cannot understand those who have advocated the strange linking of two contrary principles. To graft brotherhood onto competition is a wretched idea: it is like replacing eunuchs by hermaphrodites." The pre-Marxian Louis Blanc wanted to "reach a uniform price" determined by the State, and prevent all competition between establishments within an industry. Proudhon retorted that prices "can only be fixed by competition, that is, by the power of the consumer . . . to dispense with the services of those who overcharge . . . ." "Remove competition . . . and you deprive society of its motive force, so that it runs down like a clock with a broken spring."

Proudhon, however, did not hide from himself the evils of competition, which he described very fully in his treatise on political economy. He knew it to be a source of inequality and admitted that "in competition, victory goes to the big battalions." It is so "anarchic" (in the pejorative sense of the term) that it operates always to the benefit of private interests, necessarily engenders civil strife and, in the long run, creates oligarchies. "Competition kills competition."

In Proudhon's view, however, the absence of competition would be no less pernicious. Taking the tobacco administration,* he found that its products were too dear and its supplies inadequate simply because it had long been a monopoly free from competition. If all industries were subject to such a system, the nation would never be able to balance its income and expenditures. The competition Proudhon dreamed of was not to be the laissez-faire competition of the capitalist economic system, but competition endowed with a higher principle to "socialize" it, competition which would function on the basis of fair exchange, in a spirit of solidarity, competition which would both protect individual initiative and bring back to society the wealth which is at present diverted from it by capitalist appropriation.

It is obvious that there was something utopian in this idea. Com-

---

* A state monopoly in France. (Translator's note.)

petition and the so-called market economy inevitably produce inequality and exploitation, and would do so even if one started
from complete equality. They could not be combined with workers'
self-management unless it were on a temporary basis, as a necessary evil, until (1) a psychology of "honest exchange" had developed among the workers; (2) most important, society as a
whole had passed from conditions of shortage to the stage of
abundance, when competition would lose its purpose.

Even in such a transitional period, however, it seems desirable
that competition should be limited, as in Yugoslavia today, to the
consumer-goods sector where it has at least the one advantage of
protecting the interests of the consumer.

The libertarian communist would condemn Proudhon's version
of a collective economy as being based on a principle of conflict;
competitors would be in a position of equality at the start, only
to be hurled into a struggle which would inevitably produce
victors and vanquished, and where goods would end up by being
exchanged according to the principles of supply and demand;
"which would be to fall right back into competition and the bourgeois world." Some critics of the Yugoslav experiment from other
communist countries use much the same terms to attack it. They
feel that self-management in any form merits the same hostility
they harbor toward a competitive market economy, as if the
two ideas were basically and permanently inseparable.

CENTRALIZATION AND PLANNING

At all events, Proudhon was aware that management by workers'
associations would have to cover large units. He stressed the "need
for centralization and large units" and asked: "Do not workers'
associations for the operation of heavy industry mean large units?"
"We put economic centralization in the place of political centralization." However, his fear of authoritarian planning made him
instinctively prefer competition inspired by solidarity. Since then,
anarchist thinkers have become advocates of a libertarian and

democratic form of planning, worked out from the bottom up by the federation of self-managing enterprises.

Bakunin foresaw that self-management would open perspectives for planning on a world-wide scale:

> Workers' cooperative associations are a new historical phenomenon; today as we witness their birth we cannot foresee their future, but only guess at the immense development which surely awaits them and the new political and social conditions they will generate. It is not only possible but probable that they will, in time, outgrow the limits of today's counties, provinces, and even states to transform the whole structure of human society, which will no longer be divided into nations but into industrial units.

These would then "form a vast economic federation" with a supreme assembly at its head. With the help of "world-wide statistics, giving data as comprehensive as they are detailed and precise," it would balance supply and demand, direct, distribute, and share out world industrial production among the different countries so that crises in trade and employment, enforced stagnation, economic disaster, and loss of capital would almost certainly entirely disappear.

COMPLETE SOCIALIZATION?

There was an ambiguity in Proudhon's idea of management by the workers' associations. It was not always clear whether the self-management groups would continue to compete with capitalist undertakings—in other words, whether a socialist sector would coexist with a private sector, as is said to be the present situation in Algeria and other newly independent countries—or whether, on the other hand, production as a whole would be socialized and made subject to self-management.

Bakunin was a consistent collectivist and clearly saw the dangers of the coexistence of the two sectors. Even in association the workers cannot accumulate the necessary capital to stand up to large-scale bourgeois capital. There would also be a danger that the capitalist environment would contaminate the workers' associations so that "a new class of exploiters of the labor of the proletariat" would arise within them. Self-management contains the seeds of the full economic emancipation of the working masses, but these seeds can only germinate and grow when "capital itself, industrial establishments, raw materials, and capital equipment . . . become the collective property of workers' associations for both agricultural and industrial production, and these are freely organized and federated among themselves." "Radical, conclusive social change will only be brought about by means affecting the whole society," that is, by a social revolution which transforms private property into collective property. In such a social organization the workers would be their own collective capitalists, their own employers. Only "those things which are truly for personal use" would remain private property.

Bakunin admitted that producers' cooperatives served to accustom the workers to organizing themselves, and managing their own affairs, and were the first steps in collective working-class action, but he held that until the social revolution had been achieved such islands in the midst of the capitalist system would have only a limited effect, and he urged the workers "to think more of strikes than of cooperatives."

TRADE UNIONS

Bakunin also valued the part played by trade unions, "the natural organizations of the masses," "the only really effective weapon" the workers could use against the bourgeoisie. He thought the trade-union movement could contribute more than the ideologists to organizing the forces of the proletariat independently of bourgeois radicalism. He saw the future as the national and international organization of the workers by trade.

Trade unionism was not specially mentioned at the first congresses of the International. From the Basel Congress in 1869 onward, it became a prime issue, owing to the influence of the anarchists: after the abolition of the wage system, trade unions would become the embryo of the administration of the future; government would be replaced by councils of workers' organizations.

In 1876 James Guillaume, a disciple of Bakunin, wrote his *Idées sur l'Organisation Sociale*, in which he made self-management incorporate trade unionism. He advocated the creation of corporate federations of workers, in particular trades which would be united "not, as before, to protect their wages against the greed of the employers, but . . . to provide mutual guarantees for access to the tools of their trade, which would become the collective property of the whole corporate federation as the result of reciprocal contracts." Bakunin's view was that these federations would act as planning agencies, thus filling one of the gaps in Proudhon's plan for self-management. One thing had been lacking in his proposals the link which would unite the various producers' associations and prevent them from running their affairs egotistically, in a parochial spirit, without care for the general good or the other workers' associations. Trade unionism was to fill the gap and articulate self-management. It was presented as the agent of planning and unity among producers.

THE COMMUNES

During his early career Proudhon was entirely concerned with economic organization. His suspicion of anything political led him to neglect the problem of territorial administration. It was enough for him to say that the workers must take the place of the State without saying precisely how this would come about. In the latter years of his life he paid more attention to the political problem, which he approached from the bottom up in true anarchist style. On a local basis men were to combine among themselves into what he called a "natural group" which "constitutes itself into a city or political unit, asserting itself in unity, independence, and autonomy." "Similar groups, some distance apart, may have interests in common; it is conceivable that they may associate together and form a higher group for mutual security." At this point the anarchist thinker saw the specter of the hated State: never, never should the local groups "as they unite to safeguard their interests and develop their wealth . . . go so far as to abdicate in a sort of self-immolation at the feet of the new Moloch."

Proudhon defined the autonomous commune with some precision: it is essentially a "sovereign being" and, as such, "has the right to govern and administer itself, to impose taxes, to dispose of its property and revenue, to set up schools for its youth and appoint teachers," etc. "That is what a commune is, for that is what collective political life is . . . . It denies all restrictions, is self-limiting; all external coercion is alien to it and a menace to its survival." It has been shown that Proudhon thought self-management incompatible with an authoritarian State; similarly, the commune could not coexist with authority centralized from above:

> There is no halfway house. The commune will be sovereign or subject, all or nothing. Cast it in the best role you can; as soon as it is no longer subject to its own law, recognizes a higher authority, [and] the larger grouping . . . of which it is a member is declared to be superior . . . , it is inevitable that they will at some time disagree and come into conflict. As soon as there is a conflict the logic of power insures victory for the central authority, and this without discussion, negotiation, or trial, debate between authority and subordinate being impermissible, scandalous, and absurd.

Bakunin slotted the commune into the social organization of the future more logically than Proudhon. The associations of productive workers were to be freely allied within the communes and the communes, in their turn, freely federated among themselves. "Spontaneous life and action have been held in abeyance for centuries by the all-absorbing and monopolistic power of the State; its abdication will return them to the communes."

How would trade unionism relate to the communes? In 1880 the Courtelary district of the Jura Federation* was sure of its answer: "The organ of this local life will be a federation of trades, and this local federation will become the commune." However, those drafting the report, not fully decided on this point, raised the question: "Is it to be a general assembly of all the inhabitants,

---

* A Swiss branch of the International which had adopted Bakunin's ideas.

or delegations from the trades . . . which will draw up the constitution of the commune?" The conclusion was that there were two possible systems to be considered. Should the trade union or the commune have priority? Later, especially in Russia and Spain, this question divided the "anarcho-communists" from the "anarcho-syndicalists."

Bakunin saw the commune as the ideal vehicle for the expropriation of the instruments of production for the benefit of self-management. In the first stage of social reorganization it is the commune which will give the essential minimum to each "dispossessed" person as compensation for the goods confiscated. He described its internal organization with some precision. It will be administered by a council of elected delegates with express positive mandates; these will always be responsible to the electorate and subject to recall. The council of the commune may elect from among its number executive committees for each branch of the revolutionary administration of the commune. Dividing responsibility among so many has the advantage of involving the greatest number of the rank and file in management. It curtails the disadvantages of a system of representation in which a small number of elected delegates could take over all the duties, while the people remained almost passive in rarely convoked general assemblies. Bakunin instinctively grasped that elected councils must be "working bodies," with both regulatory and executive duties—what Lenin was later to call "democracy without parliamentarianism" in one of his libertarian moods. Again the Courtelary district made this idea more explicit:

> In order to avoid falling back into the errors of centralized and bureaucratic administration, we think that the general interests of the commune should be administered by different special commissions for each branch of activity and not by a single local administrative body . . . . This arrangement would prevent administration from taking on the character of government.

The followers of Bakunin showed no such balanced judgment of the necessary stages of historical development. In the 1880's they took the collectivist anarchists to task. In a critique of the precedent set by the Paris Commune of 1871, Kropotkin scolded the people for having "once more made use of the representative system within the Commune," for having "abdicated their own initiative in favor of an assembly of people elected more or less by chance," and he lamented that some reformers "always try to preserve this government by proxy at any price." He held that the representative system had had its day. It was the organized domination of the bourgeoisie and must disappear with it. "For the new economic era which is coming, we must seek a new form of political organization based on a principle quite different from representation." Society must find forms of political relations closer to the people than representative government, "nearer to self-government, to government of oneself by oneself."

For authoritarian or libertarian socialists, the ideal to be pursued must surely be this direct democracy which, if pressed to the limits in both economic self-management and territorial administration, would destroy the last vestiges of any kind of authority. It is certain, however, that the necessary condition for its operation is a stage of social evolution in which all workers would possess learning and skills as well as consciousness, while at the same time abundance would have taken the place of shortage. In 1880, long before Lenin, the district of Courtelary proclaimed: "The more or less democratic practice of universal suffrage will become decreasingly important in a scientifically organized society." But not before its advent.

THE DISPUTED TERM "STATE"

The reader knows by now that the anarchists refused to use the term "State" even for a transitional situation. The gap between authoritarians and libertarians has not always been very wide on this score. In the First International the collectivists, whose spokesman was Bakunin, allowed the terms "regenerate State," "new and revolutionary State," or even "socialist State" to be accepted as synonyms for "social collective." The anarchists soon saw, however, that it was rather dangerous for them to use the same word as the authoritarians while giving it a quite different meaning.

They felt that a new concept called for a new word and that the use of the old term could be dangerously ambiguous; so they ceased to give the name "State" to the social collective of the future.

The Marxists, for their part, were anxious to obtain the cooperation of the anarchists to make the principle of collective ownership triumph in the International over the last remnant of neo-Proudhonian individualism. So they were willing to make verbal concessions and agreed halfheartedly to the anarchists' proposal to substitute for the word "State" either *fédération* or *solidarisation* of communes. In the same spirit, Engels attacked his friend and compatriot August Bebel about the Gotha Programme of the German social democrats, and thought it wise to suggest that he "suppress the term 'State' throughout, using instead *Gemeinwesen,* a good old German word meaning the same as the French word 'Commune.' " At the Basel Congress of 1869, the collectivist anarchists and the Marxists had united to decide that once property had been socialized it would be developed by *communes solidarisées.* In his speech Bakunin dotted the *i*'s:

> I am voting for collectivization of social wealth, and in particular of the land, in the sense of social liquidation. By social liquidation I mean the expropriation of all who are now proprietors, by the abolition of the juridical and political State which is the sanction and sole guarantor of property as it now is. As to subsequent forms of organization . . . I favor the *solidarisation* of communes . . . with all the greater satisfaction because such *solidarisation* entails the organization of society from the bottom up.

HOW SHOULD THE PUBLIC SERVICES BE MANAGED?

The compromise which had been worked out was a long way from eliminating ambiguity, the more so since at the very same Basel Congress the authoritarian socialists had not felt shy about applauding the management of the economy by the State. The problem subsequently proved especially thorny when discussion

turned to the management of large-scale public services like railways, postal services, etc. By the Hague Congress of 1872, the
followers of Marx and those of Bakunin had parted company.
Thus the debate on public services arose in the misnamed "anti-
authoritarian" International which had survived the split. This
question created fresh discord between the anarchists and those
more or less "statist" socialists who had chosen to detach themselves from Marx and remain with the anarchists in the International.

Since such public services are national in scale, it is obvious
that they cannot be managed by the workers' associations alone,
nor by the communes alone. Proudhon tried to solve the problem
by "balancing" workers' management by some form of "public
initiative," which he did not explain fully. Who was to administer the public services? The federation of the communes,
answered the libertarians; the State, the authoritarians were
tempted to reply.

At the Brussels Congress of the International in 1874, the
Belgian socialist César de Paepe tried to bring about a compromise
between the two conflicting views. Local public services would go
to the communes to be run under the direction of the local administrative body itself, nominated by the trade unions. Public
services on a larger scale would be managed by a regional administration consisting of nominees of the federation of communes and
supervised by a regional chamber of labor, while those on a
national scale would come under the "Workers' State," that is, a
State "based on a combination of free workers' communes." The
anarchists were suspicious of this ambiguous organization but de
Paepe preferred to take this suspicion as a misunderstanding: was
it not after all a verbal quarrel? If that was so he would be content to put the word "State" aside while keeping and even extend-
ing the actual thing "under the more pleasant disguise of some
other term."

Most of the libertarians thought that the report from the
Brussels Congress amounted to a restoration of the State: they
saw the "Workers' State" turning inevitably into an "authoritarian
State." If it was only a verbal quarrel they could not see why they
should christen the new society without government by the very

name used to describe the organization which was to be abolished. At a subsequent congress at Berne, in 1876, Malatesta admitted that the public services required a unique, centralized form of organization; but he refused to have them administered from above by a State. His adversaries seemed to him to confuse the State with society, that "living organic body." In the following year, 1877, at the Universal Socialist Congress in Ghent, César de Paepe admitted that his precious Workers' State or People's State "might for a period be no more than a State of wage earners," but that "must be no more than a transitional phase imposed by circumstances," after which the nameless, urgent masses would not fail to take over the means of production and put them in the hands of the workers' associations. The anarchists were not appeased by this uncertain and distant perspective: what the State took over it would never give up.

FEDERALISM

To sum up: the future libertarian society was to be endowed with a dual structure: economic, in the form of a federation of self-managing workers' associations; administrative, in the form of a federation of the communes. The final requirement was to crown and articulate this edifice with a concept of wider scope, which might be extended to apply to the whole world: federalism.

As Proudhon's thought matured, the federalist idea was clarified and became predominant. One of his last writings bore the title *Du Principe Fédératif et de la Nécessité de Reconstituer de Parti de la Révolution* (1863) and, as previously mentioned, toward the end of his life he was more inclined to call himself a federalist than an anarchist. We no longer live in the age of small, ancient cities which, moreover, even in their time, sometimes came together on a federal basis. The problem of our time is that of administering large countries. Proudhon commented: "If the State were never to extend beyond the area of a city or commune I would leave everyone to make his own judgment, and say no more. But we must not forget that it is a matter of vast conglomerations of territory within which cities, towns, and villages can be counted by the thousand." No question of fragmenting society into microcosms. Unity is essential.

It was, however, the intention of the authoritarians to rule these local groups by the laws of "conquest," to which Proudhon retorted: "I declare to them that this is completely impossible, by virtue of the very law of unity."

> All these groups . . . are indestructible organisms . . . which can no more divest themselves of their sovereign independence than a member of the city can lose his citizenship or prerogatives as a free man . . . . All that would be achieved . . . would be the creation of an irreconcilable antagonism between the general sovereignty and each of the separate sovereignties, setting authority against authority; in other words, while supposedly developing unity one would be organizing division.

In such a system of "unitary absorption" the cities or natural groups "would always be condemned to lose their identity in the superior agglomeration, which one might call artificial." Centralization means "retaining in governmental relationship groups which are autonomous by their nature"; ". . . that is, for modern society, the true tyranny." It is a system of imperialism, communism, absolutism, thundered Proudhon, adding in one of those amalgamations of which he was a master: "All these words are synonyms."

On the other hand, unity, real unity, centralization, real centralization, would be indestructible if a bond of law, a contract of mutuality, a pact of federation were concluded between the various territorial units:

> What really centralizes a society of free men . . . is the contract. Social unity . . . is the product of the free union of citizens . . . . For a nation to manifest itself in unity, this unity must be centralized . . . in all its functions and faculties; centralization must be created from the bottom up, from the periphery to the center, and all functions must be independent and self-governing. The more numerous its foci, the stronger the centralization will be.

The federal system is the opposite of governmental centralization. The two principles of libertarianism and authoritarianism which are in perpetual conflict are destined to come to terms: "Federation resolves all the problems which arise from the need to combine liberty and authority. The French Revolution provided the foundations for a new order, the secret of which lies with its heir, the working class. This is the new order: to unite all the people in a 'federation of federations.' " This expression was not used carelessly: a universal federation would be too big; the large units must be federated between themselves. In his favorite prophetic style Proudhon declared: "The twentieth century will open the era of federations."

Bakunin merely developed and strengthened the federalist ideas of Proudhon. Like Proudhon, he acclaimed the superiority of federal unity over authoritarian unity: "When the accursed power of the State is no longer there to constrain individuals, associations, communes, provinces, or regions to live together, they will be much more closely bound, will constitute a far more viable, real, and powerful whole than what they are at present forced into by the power of the State, equally oppressive to them all." The authoritarians "are always confusing . . . formal, dogmatic, and governmental unity with a real and living unity which can only derive from the freest development of all individuals and groups, and from a federal and absolutely voluntary alliance . . . of the workers' associations in the communes and, beyond the communes, in the regions, beyond the regions, in the nations."

Bakunin stressed the need for an intermediate body between the commune and the national federal organ: the province or region, a free federation of autonomous communes. It must not, however, be thought that federalism would lead to egoism or isolation. Solidarity is inseparable from freedom: "While the communes remain absolutely autonomous, they feel . . . solidarity among themselves and unite closely without losing any of their freedom." In the modern world, moral, material, and intellectual interests have created real and powerful unity between the different parts of one nation, and between the different nations; that unity will outlive the State.

Federalism, however, is a two-edged weapon. During the French Revolution the "federalism" of the Girondins was reactionary, and the royalist school of Charles Maurras advocated it under the name of "regionalism." In some countries, like the United States, the federal constitution is exploited by those who deprive men of color of their civil rights. Bakunin thought that socialism alone could give federalism a revolutionary content. For this reason his Spanish followers showed little enthusiasm for the bourgeois federalist party of Pi y Margall, which called itself Proudhonist, and even for its "cantonalist" left wing during the brief, and abortive, episode of the republic of 1873.*

INTERNATIONALISM

The federalist idea leads logically to internationalism, that is to say, the organization of nations on a federal basis into the "large, fraternal union of mankind." Here again Bakunin showed up the bourgeois utopianism of a federal idea not based on international and revolutionary socialism. Far ahead of his time, he was a "European," as people say today; he called for and desired a United States of Europe, the only way "of making a civil war between the different peoples in the European family impossible." He was careful, however, to issue a warning against any European federation based on states "as they are at present constituted."

"No centralized, bureaucratic, and hence military State, albeit called a republic, could enter seriously and sincerely into an international federation. By its very constitution, such a State will always be an overt or covert denial of internal liberty, and hence, necessarily, a permanent declaration of war, a menace to the existence of neighboring countries." Any alliance with a reactionary State would be a "betrayal of the revolution." The United States of Europe, first, and later, of the world, can only be set up after the overthrow of the old order which rests from top to bottom on violence and the principle of authority. On the other hand, if the

---

* Pi y Margall was a minister in the period between 1873 and 1874 when a republic was briefly established in Spain. (Translator's note.) When, in January 1937, Federica Montseny, a woman anarchist who had become a minister, praised the regionalism of Pi y Margall, Gaston Leval replied that he was far from a faithful follower of Bakunin.

social revolution takes place in any one country, any foreign country which has made a revolution on the same principles should be received into a revolutionary federation regardless of existing state frontiers.

True internationalism rests on self-determination, which implies the right of secession. Following Proudhon, Bakunin propounded that "each individual, each association, commune, or province, each region and nation, has the absolute right to determine its own fate, to associate with others or not, to ally itself with whomever it will, or break any alliance, without regard to so-called historical claims or the convenience of its neighbors." "The right to unite freely and separate with the same freedom is the most important of all political rights, without which confederation will always be disguised centralization."

Anarchists, however, did not regard this principle as leading to secession or isolation. On the contrary, they held "the conviction that once the right to secede is recognized, secession will, in fact, become impossible because national units will be freely established and no longer the product of violence and historical falsehood." Then, and then only, will they become "truly strong, fruitful, and permanent."

Later, Lenin, and the early congresses of the Third International, adopted this concept from Bakunin, and the Bolsheviks made it the foundation of their policy on nationalities and of their anti-colonialist strategy—until they eventually belied it to turn to authoritarian centralization and disguised imperialism.

DECOLONIZATION

It is noteworthy that logical deduction led the originators of federalism to a prophetic anticipation of the problems of decolonization. Proudhon distinguished the unit "based on conquest" from the "rational" unit and saw that "every organization that exceeds its true limits and tends to invade or annex other organizations loses in strength what it gains in size, and moves toward dissolution." The more a city (i.e., a nation) extends its population or its territory, the nearer it comes to tyranny and, finally, disruption:

> If it sets up subsidiaries or colonies some distance away, these subsidiaries or colonies will, sooner or later, change into new cities which will remain linked to the mother city only by federation, or not at all . . . .
> When the new city is ready to support itself it will itself declare its independence: by what right should the parent city presume to treat it as a vassal, as property to be exploited?
> Thus in our time we have seen the United States emancipate itself from England: and Canada likewise in fact, if not in name; Australia set out on the road to separation by the consent, and with the approval, of the mother country. In the same way Algeria will, sooner or later, constitute itself an African France unless for abominable, selfish motives we keep it as a single unit by means of force and poverty.

Bakunin had an eye on the underdeveloped countries and doubted whether "imperialist Europe" could keep 800 million Asiatics in servitude. "Two-thirds of humanity, 800 million Asians asleep in their servitude will necessarily awaken and begin to move. But in what direction and to what end?" He declared "strong sympathy for any national uprising against any form of oppression" and commended to the subject peoples the fascinating example of the Spanish uprising against Napoleon. In spite of the fantastic disproportion between the native guerrillas and the imperial troops, the occupying power failed to put them down, and the French were driven out of Spain after a five-year struggle.

Every people "has the right to be itself and no one is entitled to impose its costume, its customs, its language, its opinions, or its laws." However, Bakunin also believed that there could be no true federalism without socialism and wished that national liberation could be achieved "as much in the economic as in the political interests of the masses" and "not with ambitious intent to set up a powerful State." Any revolution for national independence "will necessarily be against the people . . . if it is carried out without the people and must therefore depend for success on a privileged class," and will thus become "a retrogressive, disastrous, counter-revolutionary movement."

It would be regrettable if the decolonized countries were to cast off the foreign yoke only to fall into indigenous political or religious servitude. Their emancipation requires that "all faith in any divine or human authority be eradicated among the masses." The national question is historically secondary to the social question and salvation depends on the social revolution. An isolated national revolution cannot succeed. The social revolution inevitably becomes a world revolution.

Bakunin foresaw that decolonization would be followed by an ever expanding federation of revolutionary peoples: "The future lies initially with the creation of a European-American international unit. Later, much later, this great European-American nation will merge with the African and Asiatic units."

This analysis brings us straight into the middle of the twentieth century.

3

Anarchism in Revolutionary Practice

1880–1914

ANARCHISM BECOMES ISOLATED FROM THE WORKING-CLASS MOVEMENT

It is now time to examine anarchism in action. Which brings us to the eve of the twentieth century. Libertarian ideas certainly played some part in the revolutions of the nineteenth century but not an independent one. Proudhon had taken a negative attitude to the 1848 Revolution even before its outbreak. He attacked it as a *political* revolution, a bourgeois booby trap, and, indeed, much of this was true. Moreover, according to Proudhon, it was inopportune and its use of barricades and street battles was outdated, for he himself dreamed of a quite different road to victory for his panacea: *mutuelliste* collectivism. As for the Paris Commune, while it is true that it spontaneously broke away from "traditional statist centralization," it was the product of a "compromise," as Henri Lefebvre has noted, a sort of "united front" between the Proudhonists and Bakuninites on the one hand and the Jacobins and Blanquists on the other. It "boldly repudiated" the State, but Bakunin had to admit that the internationalist anarchists were a "tiny minority" in its ranks.

As a result of Bakunin's impetus, anarchism had, however, succeeded in grafting itself onto the First International—a proletarian, internationalist, apolitical, mass movement. But sometime around 1880 the anarchists began to deride "the timid International of the first period," and sought to set up in its place what Malatesta in 1884 described as the "redoubtable International," which was to be anarchist, communist, anti-religious, anti-parliamentary, and revolutionary, all at the same time. This scarecrow was very flimsy: anarchism cut itself off from the working-class movement, with the result that it deteriorated and lost its way in sectarianism and minority activism.

What caused this decline? One reason was the swiftness of industrial development and the rapid conquest of political rights by workers who then became more receptive to parliamentary reformism. It followed that the international working-class movement was taken over by politically minded, electoralist, reformist social democrats whose purpose was not the social revolution but the legal conquest of the bourgeois State and the satisfaction of short-term demands.

When they found themselves a small minority, the anarchists abandoned the idea of militancy within large popular movements. Free rein was given to utopian doctrines, combining premature anticipations and nostalgic evocations of a golden age; Kropotkin, Malatesta, and their friends turned their backs on the road opened up by Bakunin on the pretext of keeping their doctrine pure. They accused Bakunin, and anarchist literature in general, of having been "too much colored by Marxism." The anarchists turned in on themselves, organized themselves for direct action in small clandestine groups which were easily infiltrated by police informers.

Bakunin's retirement was soon followed by his death and, from 1876 on, anarchism caught the bug of adventurism and wild fantasy. The Berne Congress launched the slogan of "propaganda by the deed." Cafiero and Malatesta handed out the first lesson of action. On April 5, 1877, they directed a band of some thirty armed militants who suddenly appeared in the mountains of the Italian province of Benevento, burned the parish records of a small village, distributed the funds in the tax collector's safe to the poor, and tried to install libertarian communism on a miniature, rural, infantile scale. In the end they were tracked down, numb with cold, and yielded without resistance.

Three years later, on December 25, 1880, Kropotkin was declaiming in his journal Le Révolté: "Permanent revolt in speech, writing, by the dagger and the gun, or by dynamite . . . anything suits us that is alien to legality." Between "propaganda by the deed" and attacks on individuals, only a step remained. It was soon taken.

The defection of the mass of the working class had been one of the reasons for the recourse to terrorism, and "propaganda by the deed" did indeed make some contribution to awakening the workers from their apathy. Writing in *La Révolution Prolétarienne,* November 1937, Robert Louzon* maintained that "it was like the stroke of a gong bringing the French proletariat to its feet after the prostration into which it had been plunged by the massacres of the Commune [by the right] . . . , [and was] the prelude to the foundation of the CGT [Conféderation Général du Travail] and the mass trade-union movement of the years 1900–1910." This rather optimistic view is corrected or supplemented† by the views of Fernand Pelloutier, a young anarchist who later went over to revolutionary syndicalism: he believed the use of dynamite had deterred the workers from professing libertarian socialism, however disillusioned they might have been with parliamentary socialism; none of them dared call himself an anarchist lest he seem to opt for isolated revolt as against collective action.

The social democrats were not slow to use the weapons against the anarchists furnished by the combination of bombs and Kropotkinist utopias.

SOCIAL-DEMOCRATIC CONDEMNATION OF ANARCHISM

For many years the socialist working-class movement was divided into irreconcilable segments: while anarchism slid into terrorism combined with passive waiting for the millennium, the political

---

* *La Révolution Prolétarienne* is a French monthly; Robert Louzon a veteran revolutionary syndicalist. (Translator's note.)

† Robert Louzon pointed out to the author that from a dialectic point of view this statement and that of Pelloutier are in no way mutually exclusive: terrorism had contradictory effects on the working-class movement.

movement, more or less dishonestly claiming to be Marxist, became bogged down in "parliamentary cretinism." Pierre Monatte, an anarchist who turned syndicalist, later recalled: "The revolutionary spirit in France was dying out . . . year by year. The revolutionary ideas of Guesde were now only verbal or, worse, electoral and parliamentary; those of Jaurès simply, and very frankly, ministerial and governmental." In France, the divorce between anarchists and socialists was completed at the Le Havre Congress of 1880, when the newborn workers' party threw itself into electoral politics.

In Paris in 1889 the social democrats from various countries decided to revive the long-neglected practice of holding international socialist congresses. This opened the way for the creation of the Second International and some anarchists thought it necessary to attend the meeting. Their presence gave rise to violent incidents, since the social democrats used their superior numbers to suppress all argument from their opponents. At the Brussels Congress of 1891 the libertarians were booed and expelled. However, many working-class delegates from England, Italy, and Holland, though they were indeed reformists, withdrew in protest. The next congress was held in Zurich in 1893, and the social democrats claimed that in the future they could exclude all non-trade union organizations which did not recognize the necessity for "political action," that is to say, the conquest of bourgeois power by the ballot.

At the London Congress of 1896, a few French and Italian anarchists circumvented this exclusionary condition by getting trade unions to appoint them as delegates. This was not simply a subterfuge, for, as we shall see below, the anarchists had once more found the path of reality—they had entered the trade-union movement. But when one of them, Paul Delesalle, tried to mount the rostrum, he was thrown violently to the bottom of the steps and injured. Jaurès accused the anarchists of having transformed the trade unions into revolutionary anarchist groups and of disrupting them, just as they had come to the congress only to disrupt it, "to the great benefit of bourgeois reaction."

The German social-democratic leaders at the congress, the inveterate electoralists Wilhelm Liebknecht and August Bebel, showed themselves as savage to the anarchists as they had been in the First International. Supported by Marx's daughter, Eleanor Aveling, who regarded the anarchists as "madmen," they had their own way with the meeting and got it to pass a resolution excluding from future congresses all "anti-parliamentarians" in whatever guise they might appear.

Later, in *State and Revolution,* Lenin presented the anarchists with a bouquet which concealed some thorns. He stood up for them in relation to the social democrats, accusing the latter of having "left to the anarchists a monopoly of criticism of parliamentarianism" and of having "labeled" such criticism as "anarchist." It was hardly surprising that the proletariat of the parliamentary countries became disgusted with such socialists and more and more sympathetic to the anarchists. The social democrats had termed any effort to destroy the bourgeois State as anarchist. The anarchists "correctly described the opportunist character of the ideas of most socialist parties on the State."

According to Lenin, Marx and Proudhon were as one in desiring "the demolition of the existing machine of the State." "The opportunists are unwilling to admit the similarity between Marxism and the anarchism of Proudhon and Bakunin." The social democrats entered into debate with the anarchists in an "un-Marxist" manner. Their critique of anarchism boiled down to pure bourgeois banality: "We recognize the State, the anarchists don't." The anarchists are in a strong position to retort that this kind of social democracy is failing in its duty of providing for the revolutionary education of the workers. Lenin castigated an anti-anarchist pamphlet by the Russian social democrat Plekhanov as "very unjust to the anarchists," "sophistical," "full of vulgar argument, insinuating that there is no difference between an anarchist and a bandit."

ANARCHISTS IN THE TRADE UNIONS

In the 1890's the anarchists had reached a dead end and they were cut off from the world of the workers which had become the monopoly of the social democrats. They snuggled into little sects, barricaded themselves into ivory towers where they polished up increasingly unrealistic dogmas; or else they performed and applauded acts of individual terrorism, and let themselves be caught in a net of repression and reprisal.

Kropotkin deserves credit for being one of the first to confess his errors and to recognize the sterility of "propaganda by the deed." In a series of articles which appeared in 1890 he affirmed "that one must be with the people, who no longer want isolated acts, but want men of action inside their ranks." He warned his readers against "the illusion that one can defeat the coalition of exploiters with a few pounds of explosives." He proposed a return to mass trade unionism like that of which the First International had been the embryo and propagator: "Monster unions embracing millions of proletarians."

It was the imperative duty of the anarchists to penetrate into the trade unions in order to detach the working masses from the false socialists who were deceiving them. In 1895 an anarchist weekly, *Les Temps Nouveaux*, published an article by Fernand Pelloutier entitled "Anarchism and the Trade Unions" which expounded the new tactic. Anarchism could do very well without dynamite and must approach the masses, both to propagate anarchist ideas as widely as possible and to save the trade-union movement from the narrow corporatism in which it had become bogged down. The trade union must be a "practical school of anarchism." As a laboratory of economic struggle, detached from electoral competition and administered on anarchist lines, was not the trade union the only libertarian and revolutionary organization which could counterbalance and destroy the evil influence of the social-democratic politicians? Pelloutier linked the trade unions to the libertarian communist society which remained the ultimate objective of the anarchist: on the day when the revolution breaks out, he asked, "would they not be an almost libertarian organization, ready to succeed the existing order, thus effectively abolishing all political authority; each of its parts controlling the means of production, managing its own affairs, sovereign over itself by the free consent of its members?"

Later, at the International Anarchist Congress of 1907, Pierre

Monatte declared: "Trade unionism . . . opens up new perspectives for anarchism, too long turned in on itself." On the one hand, "trade unionism . . . has renewed anarchism's awareness of its working-class roots; on the other, the anarchists have made no small contribution to setting the working-class movement on the road to revolution and to popularizing the idea of direct action." After a lively debate, this congress adopted a compromise resolution which opened with the following statement of principle: "This International Anarchist Congress sees the trade unions both as combat units in the class struggle for better working conditions, and as associations of producers which can serve to transform capitalist society into an anarcho-communist society."

The syndicalist anarchists met with some difficulties in their efforts to draw the whole libertarian movement onto the new road they had chosen. The "pure ones" of anarchism cherished insurmountable suspicions with regard to the trade-union movement. They resented it for having its feet too firmly on the ground. They accused it of a complacent attitude toward capitalist society, of being an integral part of it, of limiting itself to short-term demands. They disputed its claim to be able to resolve the social problem single-handed. At the 1907 congress Malatesta replied sharply to Monatte, maintaining that the industrial movement was for the anarchist a means and not an end: "Trade unionism is not, and never will be, anything but a legalistic and conservative movement, unable to aim beyond—if that far!—the improvement of working conditions." The trade-union movement is made short-sighted by the pursuit of immediate gains and turns the workers away from the final struggle: "One should not ask workers to strike; but rather to continue working, for their own advantage." Malatesta ended by warning his hearers against the conservatism of trade-union bureaucracies: "In the industrial movement the official is a danger comparable only to parliamentarianism. Any anarchist who has agreed to become a permanent and salaried official of a trade union is lost to anarchism."

To this Monatte replied that the trade-union movement was certainly no more perfect than any other human institution: "Far from hiding its faults, I think it is wise to have them always in mind so as to react against them." He recognized that trade-union officialdom aroused sharp criticism, often justified. But he protested against the charge of wishing to sacrifice anarchism and the revolution to trade unionism: "As with everyone else here, anarchy is our final aim. However, because times have changed we have changed our conception of the movement and of the revolution . . . . If, instead of criticizing the past, present, or even future mistakes of trade unionism from above, the anarchists would concern themselves more intimately with its work, the dangers that lurk in trade unionism would be averted forever."

The anger of the sectarian anarchists was not entirely without cause. However, the kind of trade union of which they disapproved belonged to a past period: that which was at first purely and simply corporative, and later, the blind follower of those social-democratic politicians who had multiplied in France during the long years following the repression of the Commune. The trade unionism of class struggle, on the other hand, had been regenerated by the anarcho-syndicalists who had entered it, and it gave the "pure" anarchists the opposite cause for complaint: it claimed to produce its own ideology, to "be sufficient unto itself." Its most effective spokesman, Emile Pouget, maintained: "The trade union is superior to any other form of cohesion between individuals because the task of partial amelioration and the more decisive one of social transformation can be carried on side by side within its framework. It is precisely because the trade union answers this twofold need, . . . no longer sacrificing the present to the future or the future to the present, that the trade union stands out as the best kind of group."

The concern of the new trade unionism to emphasize and preserve its "independence" was proclaimed in a famous charter adopted by the CGT congress in Amiens in 1906. The statement was not inspired so much by opposition to anarchism as by the desire to get rid of the tutelage of bourgeois democracy and its extension in the working-class movement, social democracy. It was also felt important to preserve the cohesion of the trade-union movement when confronted with a proliferation of rival political sects, such as existed in France before "socialist unity" was established. Proudhon's work *De la Capacité Politique des Classes Ouvrières* (1865) was taken by the revolutionary syndicalists as their bible; from it they had selected for particular attention the idea of "separation": being a distinct class, the proletariat must refuse all support from the opposing class. Some anarchists, however, were shocked by the claim of trade unionism to do without their patronage. Malatesta exclaimed that it was a radically false doctrine which threatened the very existence of anarchism. Jean Grave, his faithful follower, echoed: "Trade unionism can—and must—be self-sufficient in its struggle against exploitation by the employers, but it cannot pretend to be able to solve the social problem by itself." It "is so little sufficient unto itself that the very idea of what it is, of what it should be, and of what it should do, had to come to it from outside."

In spite of these recriminations, the revolutionary ferment brought with them by the anarchist converts to trade unionism made the trade-union movement in France and the other Latin countries a power to be reckoned with in the years before the Great War. This affected not only the bourgeoisie and government, but also the social-democratic politicians who thenceforth lost most of their control over the working-class movement. The philosopher Georges Sorel considered the entry of the anarchists into the trade unions as one of the major events of his time. Anarchist doctrine had been diluted in a mass movement, only to emerge renewed and freshly tempered.

The libertarian movement was to remain impregnated with this fusion between the anarchist idea and the trade-union idea. Until 1914 the French CGT was the ephemeral product of this synthesis, but its most complete and durable product was to be the Spanish CNT (Confederación Nacional del Trabajo). It was formed in 1910, taking advantage of the disintegration of the radical party of the politician Alexandre Lerroux. One of the spokesmen of Spanish anarcho-syndicalism, Diego Abad de Santillan, did not forget to give credit to Fernand Pelloutier, to Emile Pouget, and to the other anarchists who had understood how necessary it was to begin by implanting their ideas in the economic organizations of the proletariat.

Anarchism in the Russian Revolution

Anarchism had found its second wind in revolutionary syndicalism; the Russian Revolution gave it its third. This statement may at first surprise the reader, accustomed to think of the great revolutionary movement of October 1917 as the work and domain of the Bolsheviks alone. The Russian Revolution was, in fact, a great mass movement, a wave rising from the people which passed over and submerged ideological formations. It belonged to no one, unless to the people. In so far as it was an authentic revolution, taking its impulse from the bottom upward and spontaneously producing the organs of direct democracy, it presented all the characteristics of a social revolution with libertarian tendencies. However, the relative weakness of the Russian anarchists prevented them from exploiting situations which were exceptionally favorable to the triumph of their ideas.

The Revolution was ultimately confiscated and distorted by the mastery, according to some—the cunning, according to others—of the professional revolutionary team grouped around Lenin. But this defeat of both anarchism and the authentic popular revolution was not entirely sterile for the libertarian idea. In the first place, the collective appropriation of the means of production has not again been put in question, and this safeguards the ground upon which, one day perhaps, socialism from below may prevail over state regimentation; moreover, the Russian experience has provided the occasion for some Russian and some non-Russian anarchists to learn the complex lessons of a temporary defeat—lessons of which Lenin himself seemed to have become aware on the eve of his death. In this context they could rethink the whole problem of revolution and anarchism. According to Kropotkin, echoed by Voline, it taught them, should they ever need to know, how *not* to make a revolution. Far from proving that libertarian socialism is impracticable, the Soviet experience, on the contrary, broadly confirmed the prophetic correctness of the views of the founders of anarchism and, in particular, their critique of authoritarian socialism.

A LIBERTARIAN REVOLUTION

The point of departure of the Revolution of 1917 was that of 1905, during which a new kind of revolutionary organ had come into being: the soviets. They were born in the factories of St. Petersburg during a spontaneous general strike. In the almost complete absence of a trade-union movement and tradition, the soviets filled a vacuum by coordinating the struggle of the factories on strike. The anarchist Voline was one of the small group which had the idea of setting up the first soviet, in close liaison with the workers and at their suggestion. His evidence coincides with that of Trotsky, who became president of the soviet a few months later. In his account of 1905 he wrote, without any pejorative intent—quite the contrary: "The activity of the soviet represented the organization of anarchy. Its existence and its subsequent development marked the consolidation of anarchy."

This experience had made a permanent mark upon workingclass consciousness and, when the second Russian Revolution broke out in February 1917, its leaders did not have to invent anything. The workers took over the factories spontaneously. The soviets revived on their own initiative. Once again, they took the professional revolutionaries by surprise. On Lenin's own admission, the masses of peasants and workers were "a hundred times further to the left" than the Bolsheviks. The prestige of the soviets was such that it was only in their name and at their behest that the October insurrection could be launched.

In spite of their vigor, however, they were lacking in homogeneity, revolutionary experience, and ideological preparation. This made them easy prey to political parties with uncertain revolutionary ideas. Although it was a minority organization, the Bolshevik Party was the only really organized revolutionary force which knew where it was going. It had no rivals on the extreme left in either the political or the trade-union field. It had first-class cadres at its disposal, and set in motion, as Voline admitted, "a feverish, overwhelming, fierce activity."

The party machine, however—of which Stalin was at that time an obscure ornament—had always regarded the soviets with suspicion as embarrassing competitors. Immediately after the seizure of power, the spontaneous and irresistible tendency toward the socialization of production was, at first, channeled through workers' control. A decree of November 14, 1917, legalized the participation of workers in the management of enterprises and the fixing of prices; it abolished trade secrets, and compelled the employers to publish their correspondence and their accounts. According to Victor Serge, "the leaders of the Revolution did not intend to go beyond this." In April 1918 they "still intended . . . to set up mixed companies with shares, in which the Soviet State and Russian and foreign capital would all participate." "The initiative for measures of expropriation came from the masses and not from authority."

As early as October 20, 1917, at the first Congress of Factory Councils, a motion inspired by anarchism was presented. It proposed "control over production, and that control commissions should not be simply investigative bodies, but . . . from this moment on cells of the future preparing to transfer production to the hands of the workers." "In the very early days of the October Revolution," Anna Pankratova* reported, "anarchist tendencies were the more easily and successfully manifested, because the capitalists put up the liveliest resistance to the enforcement of the decree on workers' control and actually refused workers' participation in production."

Workers' control in effect soon showed itself to be a half measure, halting and inefficient. The employers sabotaged it, concealed their stocks, removed tools, challenged or locked out the workers; sometimes they used the factory committees as simple

---

* A Bolshevik historian who later became a Stalinist.

agents or aides to management; they even thought it profitable to try to have their firms nationalized. The workers responded to these maneuvers by seizing the factories and running them for their own benefit. "We ourselves will not send the owners away," the workers said in their resolutions, "but we will take charge of production if they will not insure that the factories function." Anna Pankratova adds that, in this first period of "chaotic" and "primitive" socialization, the factory councils "frequently took over the management of factories whose owners had been dismissed or had fled."

Workers' control soon had to give place to socialization. Lenin literally did violence to his more timorous lieutenants by throwing them into the "crucible of living popular creativity," by obliging them to speak in authentic libertarian language. The basis of revolutionary reconstruction was to be workers' self-management. It alone could arouse in the masses such revolutionary enthusiasm that the impossible would become possible. When the last manual worker, any unemployed person, any cook, could see the factories, the land, the administration in the hands of associations of workers, of employees, of officials, of peasants; rationing in the hands of democratic committees, etc; all created spontaneously by the people—"when the poor see and feel that, there will be no force able to defeat the social revolution." The future seemed to be opening up for a republic of the type of the Commune of 1871, a republic of soviets.

According to Voline's account, "in order to catch the imagination of the masses, gain their confidence and their sympathy, the Bolshevik Party announced . . . slogans which had up till then been characteristic . . . of anarchism." *All power to the soviets* was a slogan which the masses intuitively understood in the libertarian sense. Peter Archinoff reported that "the workers interpreted the idea of soviet power as that of their own right to dispose of themselves socially and economically." At the Third Congress of Soviets, at the beginning of 1918, Lenin declared: "Anarchist ideas have now taken on living form." Soon after, at the Seventh Party Congress, March 6–8, he proposed for adoption theses which dealt among other things with the socialization of production administered by workers' organizations (trade unions, factory committees, etc.); the abolition of officials in charge of manual trades, of the police and the army; the equality of salaries and remuneration; the participation of all members of the soviets in management and administration of the State; the complete elimination by stages of the said State and of the use of money. At the Trade-Union Congress (spring 1918), Lenin described the factories as "self-governing communes of producers and consumers." The anarcho-syndicalist Maximoff goes so far as to maintain that "the Bolsheviks had not only abandoned the theory of the gradual withering away of the State, but Marxist ideology in general. They had become some kind of anarchists."

AN AUTHORITARIAN REVOLUTION

This audacious alignment with the instinct of the masses and their revolutionary temper may have succeeded in giving the Bolsheviks command over the revolution, but had nothing to do with their traditional ideology or their real intentions. They had been authoritarians for a long time, and were imbued with ideas of the State, of dictatorship, of centralization, of a ruling party, of management of the economy from above, of all things which were in flagrant contradiction with a really libertarian conception of soviet democracy.

State and Revolution was written on the eve of the October insurrection and mirrors the ambivalence of Lenin's thoughts. Some pages might have been written by a libertarian and, as we have seen above,* some credit at least is given to the anarchists. However, this call for a revolution from below runs parallel to a statement of the case for a revolution from above. Concepts of a hierarchical, centralized state system are not half concealed afterthoughts but, on the contrary, are frankly expressed: the State will survive the conquest of power by the proletariat and will wither away only after a transitional period. How long is this purgatory to last? This is not concealed; we are told rather with

---

* See page 77.

relief than with regret that the process will be "slow," and "of long duration." Under the guise of soviet power, the revolution will bring forth the "proletarian State," or "dictatorship of the proletariat"; the writer even lets slip the expression "bourgeois State without the bourgeoisie," just when he is revealing his inmost thoughts. This omnivorous State surely intends to take everything over.

Lenin took a lesson from contemporary German state capitalism, the *Kriegswirtschaft* (war economy). Another of his models was the organization of modern large-scale industry by capitalism, with its "iron discipline." He was particularly entranced by a state monopoly such as the posts and telegraphs and exclaimed: "What an admirably perfected mechanism! The whole of economic life organized like the postal services, . . . that is the State, that is the economic base which we need." To seek to do without "authority" and "subordination" is an "anarchist dream," he concluded. At one time he had waxed enthusiastic over the idea of entrusting production and exchange to workers' associations and to self-management. But that was a misdeal. Now he did not hide his magic prescription: all citizens becoming "employees and workers of one universal single state trust," the whole of society converted into "one great office and one great factory." There would be soviets, to be sure, but under the control of the workers' party, a party whose historic task it is to "direct" the proletariat.

The most clear-minded Russian anarchists were not misled by this view. At the peak of Lenin's libertarian period they were already warning the workers to be on their guard: in their journal, *Golos Truda* (The Voice of Labor), in the last months of 1917 and early in 1918 Voline wrote the following prophetic warning:

Once they have consolidated and legalized their power, the Bolsheviks—who are socialists, politicians, and believers in the State, that is to say, centralist and authoritarian men of action—will begin to arrange the life of the country and the people by governmental and dictatorial means imposed from the centers . . . . Your soviets . . . will gradually become simply executive organs of the will of the central government. . . . An authoritarian political state apparatus will be set up and, acting from above, it will seek to crush everything with its iron fist . . . Woe betide anyone who is not in agreement with the central authority.

"*All power to the soviets* will become in effect the authority of the party leaders."

It was Voline's view that it was the increasingly anarchist tendencies of the masses which obliged Lenin to turn away from his original path for a time. He would allow the State, authority, the dictatorship, to remain only for an hour, for a short moment. And then would come "anarchism." "But, good God, do you not foresee . . . what citizen Lenin will say when real power has been consolidated and it has become possible not to listen any more to the voice of the masses?" Then he will come back to the beaten path. He will create "a Marxist State," of the most complete type.

It would, of course, be risky to maintain that Lenin and his team consciously set a trap for the masses. There was more doctrinal dualism in them than deliberate duplicity. The contradiction between the two poles of their thought was so obvious, so flagrant, that it was to be foreseen that it would soon impinge upon events. Either the anarchist trend and the pressure of the masses would oblige the Bolsheviks to forget the authoritarian aspect of their concepts, or, on the contrary, the consolidation of their power, coinciding with the exhaustion of the people's revolutionary upsurge, would lead them to put aside their transitory anarchist thoughts.

A new factor then made its appearance, disturbing the balance of the issues in question: the terrible circumstances of the civil war and the foreign intervention, the disorganization of transport, the shortage of technicians. These things drove the Bolshevik leaders to emergency measures, to dictatorship, to centralization, and to recourse to the "iron fist." The anarchists, however, denied that these were the result simply of objective causes external to the Revolution. In their opinion they were due in part to the internal logic of the authoritarian ideas of Bolshevism, to the weakness of an overcentralized and excessively bureaucratic authority. According to Voline, it was, among other things, the incompetence of the State, and its desire to direct and control everything, that made it incapable of reorganizing the economic life of the country and led to a real "breakdown"; that is, to the paralysis of industry, the ruin of agriculture, and the destruction of all connections between the various branches of the economy.

As an example, Voline told the story of the former Nobel oil refinery at Petrograd. It had been abandoned by its owners and its 4,000 workers decided to operate it collectively. They addressed themselves to the Bolshevik government in vain. Then they tried to make the plant work on their own initiative. They divided themselves into mobile groups and tried to find fuel, raw materials, outlets, and means of transport. With regard to the latter they had actually begun discussions with their comrades among the railwaymen. The government became angry, feeling that its responsibility to the country prevented it from allowing each factory to act independently. The workers' council persisted and called a general assembly of the workers. The People's Commissar of Labor took the trouble to give a personal warning to the workers against a "serious act of insubordination." He castigated their attitude as "anarchistic and egotistical." He threatened them with dismissal without compensation. The workers retorted that they were not asking for any privileges: the government should let the workers and peasants all over the country act in the same way. All in vain, the government stuck to its point of view and the factory was closed.

One Communist confirms Voline's analysis: Alexandra Kollontay. In 1921 she complained that numerous examples of workers' initiative had come to grief amid endless paperwork and useless administrative discussions: "How much bitterness there is among the workers . . . when they see what they could have achieved if they had been given the right and the freedom to act. . . . Initiative becomes weak and the desire for action dies down."

In fact the power of the soviets only lasted a few months, from October 1917 to the spring of 1918. The factory councils were very soon deprived of their power, on the pretext that self-management did not take account of the "rational" needs of the economy, that it involved an egoism of enterprises competing

one with the other, grasping for scarce resources, wanting to survive at any price even if other factories were more important "for
the State" and better equipped. In brief, according to Anna Pankratova, the situation was moving toward a fragmentation of the
economy into "autonomous producers' federations of the kind
dreamed of by the anarchists." No doubt the budding workers'
self-management was not above reproach. It had tried, painfully
and tentatively, to create new forms of production which had
no precedent in world history. It had certainly made mistakes and
taken wrong turns. That was the price of apprenticeship. As
Alexandra Kollontay maintained, communism could not be "born
except by a process of practical research, with mistakes perhaps,
but starting from the creative forces of the working class itself."

The leaders of the Party did not hold this view. They were only
too pleased to take back from the factory committees the power
which they had not in their heart of hearts been happy to hand
over. As early as 1918, Lenin stated his preference for the "single
will" in the management of enterprises. The workers must obey
"unconditionally" the single will of the directors of the work
process. All the Bolshevik leaders, Kollontay tells us, were "skeptical with regard to the creative abilities of workers' collectives."
Moreover, the administration was invaded by large numbers of
petty bourgeois, left over from old Russian capitalism, who had
adapted themselves all too quickly to institutions of the soviet
type, and had got themselves into responsible positions in the
various commissariats, insisting that economic management should
be entrusted to them and not to workers' organizations.

The state bureaucracy played an increasing role in the economy.
From December 5, 1917, on, industry was put under a Supreme
Economic Council, responsible for the authoritarian coordination
of the activity of all organs of production. From May 26 to
June 4, 1918, the Congress of Economic Councils met and decided that the directorate of each enterprise should be composed
of members two-thirds of whom would be nominated by the
regional councils or the Supreme Economic Council and only one-
third elected by workers on the spot. A decree of May 28, 1918,
extended collectivization to industry as a whole but, by the same
token, transformed the spontaneous socializations of the first

months of the revolution into nationalizations. The Supreme Economic Council was made responsible for the administration of the nationalized industries. The directors and technical staff were to remain at their posts as appointees of the State. At the Second Congress of the Supreme Economic Council at the end of 1918, the factory councils were roundly trounced by the committee reporter for trying to direct the factories in the place of the board of directors.

For the sake of appearances, elections to factory committees continued to take place, but a member of the Communist cell read out a list of candidates drawn up in advance and voting was by show of hands in the presence of the armed "Communist guards" of the enterprise. Anyone who declared his opposition to the proposed candidates became subject to economic sanctions (wage cuts, etc.). As Peter Archinoff reported, there remained a single omnipresent master—the State. Relations between the workers and this new master became similar to those which had previously existed between labor and capital.

The functions of the soviets had become purely nominal. They were transformed into institutions of government power. "You must become basic cells of the State," Lenin told the Congress of Factory Councils on June 27, 1918. As Voline expressed it, they were reduced to the role of "purely administrative and executive organs responsible for small, unimportant local matters and entirely subject to 'directives' from the central authorities: government and the leading organs of the Party." They no longer had "even the shadow of power." At the Third Trades-Union Congress (April 1920), the committee reporter, Lozovosky, admitted: "We have abandoned the old methods of workers' control and we have preserved only the principle of state control." From now on this "control" was to be exercised by an organ of the State: the Workers' and Peasants' Inspectorate.

The industrial federations which were centralist in structure had, in the first place, helped the Bolsheviks to absorb and subjugate the factory councils which were federalist and libertarian in their nature. From April 1, 1918, the fusion between the two types of organization was an accomplished fact. From then on the trade unions played a disciplinary role under the supervision of the Party. The union of workers in the heavy metal industries of Petrograd forbade "disruptive initiatives" from the factory councils and objected to their "most dangerous" tendency to put this or that enterprise into the hands of the workers. This was said to be the worst way of imitating production cooperatives, "the idea of which had long since been bankrupt" and which would "not fail to transform themselves into capitalist undertakings." "Any enterprise abandoned or sabotaged by an industrialist, the product of which was necessary to the national economy, was to be placed under the control of the State." It was "not permissible" that the workers should take over such enterprises without the approval of the trade-union organization.

After this preliminary take-over operation the trade unions were, in their turn, tamed, deprived of any autonomy, purged; their congresses were postponed, their members arrested, their organizations disbanded or merged into larger units. At the end of this process any anarcho-syndicalist tendency had been wiped out, and the trade-union movement was completely subordinated to the State and the single party.

The same thing happened with regard to consumers' cooperatives. In the early stages of the Revolution they had arisen everywhere, increased in numbers, and federated with each other. Their offense, however, was that they were outside the control of the Party and a certain number of social democrats (Mensheviks) had infiltrated them. First, local shops were deprived of their supplies and means of transport on the pretext of "private trade" and "speculation," or even without any pretext at all. Then, all free cooperatives were closed at one stroke and state cooperatives set up bureaucratically in their place. The decree of March 20, 1919, absorbed the consumer cooperatives into the Commissariat of Food Supplies and the industrial producer cooperatives into the Supreme Economic Council. Many members of cooperatives were thrown into prison.

The working class did not react either quickly or vigorously enough. It was dispersed, isolated in an immense, backward, and for the most part rural country exhausted by privation and revolutionary struggle, and, still worse, demoralized. Finally, its best members had left for the fronts of the civil war or had been absorbed into the party and government apparatus. Nevertheless, quite a number of workers felt themselves more or less done out of the fruits of their revolutionary victories, deprived of their rights, subjected to tutelage, humiliated by the arrogance and arbitrary power of the new masters; and these became aware of the real nature of the supposed "proletarian State." Thus, during the summer of 1918, dissatisfied workers in the Moscow and Petrograd factories elected delegates from among their number, trying in this way to oppose their authentic "delegate councils" to the soviets of enterprises already captured by authority. Kollontay bears witness that the worker felt sore and understood that he had been pushed aside. He could compare the life style of the soviet functionaries with the way in which he lived—he upon whom the "dictatorship of the proletariat" was based, at least in theory.

By the time the workers really saw the light it was too late. Power had had the time to organize itself solidly and had at its disposal repressive forces fully able to break any attempted autonomous action on the part of the masses. According to Voline, a bitter but unequal struggle lasted some three years, and was entirely unknown outside Russia. In this a working-class vanguard opposed a state apparatus determined to deny the division which had developed between itself and the masses. From 1919 to 1921, strikes increased in the large cities, in Petrograd especially, and even in Moscow. They were severely repressed, as we shall see further on.

Within the directing Party itself a "Workers' Opposition" arose which demanded a return to the democracy of the soviets and self-management. At the Tenth Party Congress in March 1921, one of its spokesmen, Alexandra Kollontay, distributed a pamphlet asking for freedom of initiative and organization for the trade unions and for a "congress of producers" to elect a central administrative organ for the national economy. The brochure was confiscated and banned. Lenin persuaded almost the whole congress to vote for a resolution identifying the theses of the Workers' Opposition with "petty-bourgeois and anarchist deviations": the "syndicalism," the "semi-anarchism" of the oppositionists was in his eyes a "direct danger" to the monopoly of power exercised by the Party in the name of the proletariat. From then on all opposition within the Party was forbidden and the way was open to "totalitarianism," as was admitted by Trotsky years later.

The struggle continued within the central leadership of the trade unions. Tomsky and Riazanov were excluded from the Presidium and sent into exile, because they had stood for trade unions independent of the Party. The leader of the workers' opposition, Shlyapnikov, met the same fate, and was soon followed by the prime mover of another opposition group: G. I. Miasnikov, a genuine worker who had put the Grand Duke Michael to death in 1917. He had been a party member for fifteen years and, before the revolution, spent more than seven years in prison and seventy-five days on a hunger strike. In November 1921, he dared to state in a pamphlet that the workers had lost confidence in the Communists, because the Party no longer had a common language with the rank and file and was now using against the working class the repressive measures brought in against the bourgeoisie between 1918 and 1920.

THE PART PLAYED
BY THE ANARCHISTS

What part did the Russian anarchists play in this drama in which a libertarian-style revolution was transmuted into its opposite? Russia had no libertarian traditions and it was in foreign lands that Bakunin and Kropotkin became anarchists. Neither played a militant anarchist role inside Russia at any time. Up to the time of the 1917 Revolution, only a few copies of short extracts from their writings had appeared in Russia, clandestinely and with great difficulty. There was nothing anarchist in the social, socialist, and revolutionary education of the Russians. On the contrary, as Voline told us, "advanced Russian youth were reading literature which always presented socialism in a statist form." People's minds were soaked in ideas of government, having been contaminated by German social democracy.

The anarchists "were a tiny handful of men without influence," at the most a few thousand. Voline reported that their movement was "still far too small to have any immediate, concrete effect on events." Moreover, most of them were individualist intellectuals not much involved in the working-class movement. Voline was an exception, as was Nestor Makhno, who could move the hearts of the masses in his native Ukraine. In Makhno's memoirs he passed the severe judgment that "Russian anarchism lagged behind events or even functioned completely outside them."

However, this judgment seems to be less than fair. The anarchists played a far from negligible part in events between the February and October revolutions. Trotsky admitted this more than once in his *History of the Russian Revolution.* "Brave" and "active," though few in numbers, they were a principled opposition in the Constituent Assembly at a time when the Bolsheviks had not yet turned anti-parliamentary. They put out the call "all power to the soviets" long before Lenin's party did so. They inspired the movement for the spontaneous socialization of housing, often against the will of the Bolsheviks. Anarcho-syndicalist activists played a part in inducing workers to take over the factories, even before October.

During the revolutionary days that brought Kerensky's bourgeois republic to an end, the anarchists were in the forefront of the military struggle, especially in the Dvinsk regiment commanded by old libertarians like Grachoff and Fedotoff. This force dislodged the counter-revolutionary "cadets." Aided by his detachment, the anarchist Gelezniakov disbanded the Constituent Assembly: the Bolsheviks only ratified the accomplished fact. Many partisan detachments were formed or led by anarchists (Mokrooussoff, Cherniak, and others), and fought unremittingly against the White armies between 1918 and 1920.

Scarcely a major city was without an anarchist or anarcho-syndicalist group, spreading a relatively large amount of printed matter—papers, periodicals, leaflets, pamphlets, and books. There were two weeklies in Petrograd and a daily in Moscow, each appearing in 25,000 copies. Anarchist sympathizers increased as the Revolution deepened and then moved away from the masses. The French captain Jacques Sadoul, on a mission in Russia, wrote in a report dated April 6, 1918: "The anarchist party is the most active, the most militant of the opposition groups and probably the most popular . . . . The Bolsheviks are anxious." At the end of 1918, according to Voline, "this influence became so great that the Bolsheviks, who could not accept criticism, still less opposition, became seriously disturbed." Voline reports that for the Bolshevik authorities "it was equivalent . . . to suicide to tolerate anarchist propaganda. They did their best first to prevent, and then to forbid, any manifestation of libertarian ideas and finally suppressed them by brute force."

The Bolshevik government "began by forcibly closing the offices of libertarian organizations, and forbidding the anarchists from taking part in any propaganda or activity." In Moscow on the night of April 12, 1918, detachments of Red Guards, armed to the teeth, took over by surprise twenty-five houses occupied by the anarchists. The latter, thinking that they were being attacked by White Guards, replied with gunfire. According to Voline, the authorities soon went on to "more violent measures: imprisonment, outlawing, and execution." "For four years this conflict was to keep the Bolshevik authorities on their toes . . . until the libertarian trend was finally crushed by military measures (at the end of 1921)."

The liquidation of the anarchists was all the easier since they had divided into two factions, one of which refused to be tamed while the other allowed itself to be domesticated. The latter regarded "historical necessity" as justification for making a gesture of loyalty to the regime and, at last temporarily, approving its dictatorial actions. They considered a victorious end to the civil war and the crushing of the counter-revolution to be the first necessities.

The more intransigent anarchists regarded this as a short-sighted tactic. For the counter-revolutionary movements were being fed by the bureaucratic impotence of the government apparatus and the disillusionment and discontent of the people. Moreover, the authorities ended up by making no distinction between the active wing of the libertarian revolution which was disputing its methods of control, and the criminal activities of its right-wing adversaries. To accept dictatorship and terror was a suicidal policy for the anarchists who were themselves to become its victims. Finally, the conversion of the so-called soviet anarchists made the crushing of those other, irreconcilable, ones easier, for they were treated as "false" anarchists, irresponsible and unrealistic dreamers, stupid muddlers, madmen, sowers of division, and, finally, counter-revolutionary bandits.

Victor Serge was the most brilliant, and therefore considered the most authoritative, of the converted anarchists. He worked for the regime and published a pamphlet in French which attempted to defend it against anarchist criticism. The book he wrote later, *L'An 1 de la Révolution Russe*, is largely a justification of the liquidation of the soviets by Bolshevism. The Party—or rather its élite leadership—is presented as the brains of the working class. It is up to the duly selected leader of the vanguard to discover what the proletariat can and must do. Without them, the masses organized in soviets would be no more than "a sprinkling of men with confused aspirations shot through with gleams of intelligence."

Victor Serge was certainly too clear-minded to have any illusions about the real nature of the central Soviet power. But this power was still haloed with the prestige of the first victorious proletarian revolution; it was loathed by world counter-revolution; and that was one of the reasons—the most honorable—why Serge and many other revolutionaries saw fit to put a padlock on their tongues. In the summer of 1921 the anarchist Gaston Leval came to Moscow in the Spanish delegation to the Third Congress of the Communist International. In private, Serge confided to him that "the Communist Party no longer practices the dictatorship of the proletariat but dictatorship *over* the proletariat." Returning to France, Leval published articles in *Le Libertaire*, using well-documented facts, and placing side by side what Victor Serge had told him confidentially and his public statements, which he described as "conscious lies." In *Living My Life*, the great American anarchist Emma Goldman was no kinder to Victor Serge, whom she had seen in action in Moscow.

THE MAKHNOVTCHINA

It had been relatively easy to liquidate the small, weak nuclei of anarchists in the cities, but things were different in the Ukraine, where the peasant Nestor Makhno had built up a strong rural anarchist organization, both economic and military. Makhno was born of poor Ukrainian peasants and was twenty years old in 1919. As a child, he had seen the 1905 Revolution and later became an anarchist. The Czarist regime sentenced him to death, commuted to eight years' imprisonment, which was spent, more often than not in irons, in Boutirki prison, the only school he was ever to attend. He filled at least some of the gaps in his education with the help of a fellow-prisoner, Peter Archinoff.

Immediately after the October Revolution, Makhno took the initiative in organizing masses of peasants into an autonomous region, a roughly circular area 480 by 400 miles, with seven million inhabitants. Its southern end reached the Sea of Azov at the port of Berdiansk, and it was centered in Gulyai-Polyé, a large town of 20,000 to 30,000 people. This was a traditionally rebellious region which had seen violent disturbances in 1905.

The story began when the German and Austrian armies of occupation imposed a right-wing regime which hastened to return to their former owners the lands which had been seized by revolutionary peasants. The land workers put up an armed defense of their new conquests. They resisted reaction but also the untimely intrusion of Bolshevik commissars, and their excessive levies. This vast *Jacquerie** was inspired by a "lover of justice," a sort of anarchist Robin Hood called "Father" Makhno by the peasants. His first feat of arms was the capture of Gulyai-Polyé in mid-September 1918. The armistice of November 11, however, led to the withdrawal of the Austro-German occupation forces, and gave Makhno a unique opportunity to build up reserves of arms and supplies.

For the first time in history, the principles of libertarian com-

---

* *Jacquerie* was the name given to the French peasant revolt of 1358 (from *Jacques*, the nickname of the French peasant). (Translator's note.)

munism were applied in the liberated Ukraine, and self-management was put into force as far as possible in the circumstances of the civil war. Peasants united in "communes" or "free-work soviets," and communally tilled the land for which they had fought with the former owners. These groups respected the principles of equality and fraternity. Each man, woman, or child had to work in proportion to his or her strength, and comrades elected to temporary managerial functions subsequently returned to their regular work alongside the other members of the communes.

Each soviet was simply the executive of the will of the peasants in the locality from which it had been elected. Production units were federated into districts, and districts into regions. The soviets were integrated into a general economic system based on social equality; they were to be independent of any political party. No politician was to dictate his will to them under cover of soviet power. Members had to be authentic workers at the service of the laboring masses.

When the Makhnovist partisans moved into an area they put up posters reading: "The freedom of the workers and peasants is their own, and not subject to any restriction. It is up to the workers and peasants themselves to act, to organize themselves, to agree among themselves in all aspects of their lives, as they themselves see fit and desire . . . . The Makhnovists can do no more than give aid and counsel . . . . In no circumstances can they, nor do they wish to, govern."

When, in 1920, Makhno's men were brought to negotiate with the Bolsheviks, they did so as their equals, and concluded an ephemeral agreement with them, to which they insisted that the following appendix be added: "In the area where the Makhnovist army is operating the worker and peasant population shall create its own free institutions for economic and political self-administration; these institutions shall be autonomous and linked federally by agreements with the governing organs of the Soviet Republics." The Bolshevik negotiators were staggered and separated the appendix from the agreement in order to refer it to Moscow where of course, it was, considered "absolutely inadmissible."

One of the relative weaknesses of the Makhnovist movement was its lack of libertarian intellectuals, but it did receive some intermittent aid from outside. This came first from Kharkov and Kursk where the anarchists, inspired by Voline, had in 1918 formed a union called *Nabat* (the tocsin). In 1919 they held a congress at which they declared themselves "categorically and definitely opposed to any form of participation in the soviets, which have become purely political bodies, organized on an authoritarian, centralized, statist basis." The Bolshevik government regarded this statement as a declaration of war and the Nabat was forced to give up all its activities. Later, in July, Voline got through to Makhno's headquarters and joined with Peter Archinoff to take charge of the cultural and educational side of the movement. He presided at the congress held in October at Alexandrovsk, where the "General Theses" setting out the doctrine of the "free soviets" were adopted.

Peasant and partisan delegates took part in these congresses. In fact, the civil organization was an extension of a peasant army of insurrection, practicing guerrilla tactics. This army was remarkably mobile, covering as much as 160 miles in a day, thanks not only to its cavalry but also to its infantry, which traveled in light horse-drawn carts with springs. This army was organized on a specifically libertarian, voluntary basis. The elective principle was applied at all levels and discipline freely agreed to: the rules of the latter were drawn up by commissions of partisans, then validated by general assemblies, and were strictly observed by all.

Makhno's *franc-tireurs* gave the White armies of intervention plenty of trouble. The units of Bolshevik Red Guards, for their part, were not very effective. They fought only along the railways and never went far from their armored trains, to which they withdrew at the first reverse, sometimes without taking on board all their own combatants. This did not give much confidence to the peasants who were short of arms and isolated in their villages and so would have been at the mercy of the counter-revolutionaries. Archinoff, the historian of the Makhnovtchina, wrote that "the honor of destroying Denikin's counter-revolution in the autumn of 1919 is principally due to the anarchist insurgents."

But after the units of Red Guards had been absorbed into the Red Army, Makhno persisted in refusing to place his army under the supreme command of the Red Army chief, Trotsky. That great revolutionary therefore believed it necessary to turn upon the insurrectionary movement. On June 4, 1919, he drafted an order banning the forthcoming Makhnovist congress, accusing them of standing out against Soviet power in the Ukraine. He characterized participation in the congress as an act of "high treason" and called for the arrest of the delegates. He refused to give arms to Makhno's partisans, failing in his duty of assisting them, and subsequently accused them of "betrayal" and of allowing themselves to be beaten by the White troups. The same procedure was followed eighteen years later by the Spanish Stalinists against the anarchist brigades.

The two armies, however, came to an agreement again, on two occasions, when the extreme danger caused by the intervention required them to act together. This occurred first in March 1919, against Denikin, the second during the summer and autumn of 1920, before the menace of the White forces of Wrangel which were finally destroyed by Makhno. But as soon as the supreme danger was past the Red Army returned to military operations against the partisans of Makhno, who returned blow for blow.

At the end of November 1920 those in power went so far as to prepare an ambush. The Bolsheviks invited the officers of the Crimean Makhnovist army to take part in a military council. There they were immediately arrested by the Cheka, the political police, and shot while their partisans were disarmed. At the same time a regular offensive was launched against Gulyai-Polyé. The increasingly unequal struggle between libertarians and authoritarians continued for another nine months. In the end, however, overcome by more numerous and better equipped forces, Makhno had to give up the struggle. He managed to take refuge in Rumania in August 1921, and later reached Paris, where he died much later of disease and poverty. This was the end of the epic story of the Makhnovtchina. According to Peter Archinoff, it was the prototype of an independent movement of the working masses and hence a source of future inspiration for the workers of the world.

KRONSTADT

In February-March 1921, the Petrograd workers and the sailors of the Kronstadt fortress were driven to revolt, the aspirations which inspired them being very similar to those of the Makhnovist revolutionary peasants.

The material conditions of urban workers had become intolerable through lack of foodstuffs, fuel, and transport, and any expression of discontent was being crushed by a more and more dictatorial and totalitarian regime. At the end of February strikes broke out in Petrograd, Moscow, and several other large industrial centers. The workers demanded bread and liberty; they marched from one factory to another, closing them down, attracting new contingents of workers into their demonstrations. The authorities replied with gunfire, and the Petrograd workers in turn by a protest meeting attended by 10,000 workers. Kronstadt was an island naval base forty-eight miles from Petrograd in the Gulf of Finland which was frozen during the winter. It was populated by sailors and several thousand workers employed in the naval arsenals. The Kronstadt sailors had been in the vanguard of the revolutionary events of 1905 and 1917. As Trotsky put it, they had been the "pride and glory of the Russian Revolution." The civilian inhabitants of Kronstadt had formed a free commune, relatively independent of the authorities. In the center of the fortress an enormous public square served as a popular forum holding as many as 30,000 persons.

In 1921 the sailors certainly did not have the same revolutionary makeup and the same personnel as in 1917; they had been drawn from the peasantry far more than their predecessors; but the militant spirit had remained and as a result of their earlier performance they retained the right to take an active part in workers' meetings in Petrograd. When the workers of the former capital went on strike they sent emissaries who were driven back by the forces of order. During two mass meetings held in the main square they took up as their own the demands of the strikers.

Sixteen thousand sailors, workers, and soldiers attended the second meeting held on March 1, as did the head of state, Kalinin, president of the central executive. In spite of his presence they passed a resolution demanding that the workers, Red soldiers, and sailors of Petrograd, Kronstadt, and the Petrograd province be called together during the next ten days in a conference independent of the political parties. They also called for the abolition of "political officers," asked that no political party should have privileges, and that the Communist shock detachments in the army and "Communist guards" in the factories should be disbanded.

It was indeed the monopoly of power of the governing party which they were attacking. The Kronstadt rebels dared to call this monopoly an "usurpation." Let the angry sailors speak for themselves, as we skim through the pages of the official journal of this new commune, the *Izvestia* of Kronstadt. According to them, once it had seized power the Communist Party had only one concern: to keep it by fair means or foul. It had lost contact with the masses, and proved its inability to get the country out of a state of general collapse. It had become bureaucratic and lost the confidence of the workers. The soviets, having lost their real power, had been meddled with, taken over, and manipulated, the trade unions were being made instruments of the State. An omnipotent police apparatus weighed on the people, enforcing its laws by gunfire and the use of terror. Economic life had become not the promised socialism, based on free labor, but a harsh state capitalism. The workers were simply wage earners under this national trust, exploited just as before. The irreverent men of Kronstadt went so far as to express doubt about the infallibility of the supreme leaders of the revolution. They mocked Trotsky, and even Lenin, irreverently. Their immediate demands were the restoration of all freedoms and free elections to all the organs of soviet democracy, but beyond this they were looking to a more distant objective with a clearly anarchist content: a "third revolution."

The rebels did, however, intend to keep within the framework of the Revolution and undertook to watch over the achievements of the social revolution. They proclaimed that they had nothing in common with those who would have wished to "return to the knout of Czarism," and though they did not conceal their intention of depriving the "Communists" of power, this was not to be for the purpose of "returning the workers and peasants to slavery." Moreover, they did not cut off all possibility of cooperation with the regime, still hoping "to be able to find a common language." Finally, the freedom of expression they were demanding was not to be for just anybody, but only for sincere believers in the Revolution: anarchists and "left socialists" (a formula which would exclude social democrats or Mensheviks).

The audacity of Kronstadt was much more than a Lenin or a Trotsky could endure. The Bolshevik leaders had once and for all identified the Revolution with the Communist Party, and anything which went against this myth must, in their eyes, appear as "counter-revolutionary." They saw the whole of Marxist-Leninist orthodoxy in danger. Kronstadt frightened them the more, since they were governing in the name of the proletariat and, suddenly, their authority was being disputed by a movement which they knew to be authentically proletarian. Lenin, moreover, held the rather simplistic idea that a Czarist restoration was the only alternative to the dictatorship of his own party. The statesmen of the Kremlin in 1921 argued in the same way as those, much later, in the autumn of 1956: Kronstadt was the forerunner of Budapest.

Trotsky, the man with the "iron fist," undertook to be personally responsible for the repression. "If you persist, you will be shot down from cover like partridges," he announced to the "mutineers." The sailors were treated as "White Guardists," accomplices of the interventionist Western powers, and of the "Paris Bourse." They were to be reduced to submission by force of arms. It was in vain that the anarchists Emma Goldman and Alexander Berkman, who had found asylum in the fatherland of the workers after being deported from the United States, sent a pathetic letter to Zinoviev, insisting that the use of force would do "incalculable damage to the social revolution" and adjuring the "Bolshevik comrades" to settle the conflict through fraternal negotiation. The Petrograd workers could not come to the aid of Kronstadt because they were already terrorized, and subject to martial law.

An expeditionary force was set up composed of carefully hand-picked troops, for many Red soldiers were unwilling to fire on their class brothers. This force was put under the command of a former Czarist officer, the future Marshall Tukachevsky. The bombardment of the fortress began on March 7. Under the heading "Let the world know!" the besieged inhabitants launched a last appeal: "May the blood of the innocent be on the head of the Communists, mad, drunk and enraged with power. Long live the power of the soviets!" The attacking force moved across the frozen Gulf of Finland on March 18 and quelled the "rebellion" in an orgy of killing.

The anarchists had played no part in this affair. However, the revolutionary committee of Kronstadt had invited two libertarians to join it: Yarchouk (the founder of the Kronstadt soviet of 1917) and Voline; in vain, for they were at the time imprisoned by the Bolsheviks. Ida Mett, historian of the Kronstadt revolt (in *La Commune de Cronstadt*), commented that "the anarchist influence was brought to bear only to the extent to which anarchism itself propagated the idea of workers' democracy." The anarchists did not play any direct part in events, but they associated themselves with them. Voline later wrote: "Kronstadt was the first entirely independent attempt of the people to free themselves of all control and carry out the social revolution: this attempt was made directly, . . . by the working masses themselves, without 'political shepherds,' without 'leaders,' or 'tutors.' Alexander Berkman added: "Kronstadt blew sky high the myth of the proletarian State; it proved that the dictatorship of the Communist Party and the Revolution were really incompatible."

[handwritten margin note: anarchists @ Kronstadt]

ANARCHISM LIVING AND DEAD

Although the anarchists played no direct part in the Kronstadt rising, the regime took advantage of crushing it to make an end of an ideology which continued to frighten them. A few weeks earlier, on February 8, the aged Kropotkin had died on Russian soil, and his remains had been given an imposing funeral, which was followed by an immense convoy of about 100,000 people. Over the heads of the crowd, among the red flags, one could see the black banners of the anarchist groups inscribed in letters of fire: "Where there is authority there is no freedom." According to Kropotkin's biographers, this was "the last great demonstration against Bolshevik tyranny, and many took part more to demand freedom than to praise the great anarchist."

Hundreds of anarchists were arrested after Kronstadt, and only a few months later, the libertarian Fanny Baron and eight of her comrades were shot in the cellars of the Cheka prison in Moscow. Militant anarchism had received a fatal blow. But outside Russia, the anarchists who had lived through the Russian Revolution undertook an enormous labor of criticism and doctrinal revision which reinvigorated libertarian thought and made it more concrete. As early as September 1920, the congress of the Confederation of Anarchist Organizations of the Ukraine, Nabat, had categorically rejected the expression "dictatorship of the proletariat," seeing that it led inevitably to dictatorship over the masses by that fraction of the proletariat entrenched in the Party, by officials, and a handful of leaders. Just before he died Kropotkin had issued a "Message to the Workers of the West" in which he sorrowfully denounced the rise of a "formidable bureaucracy": "It seems to me that this attempt to build a communist republic on the basis of a strongly centralized state, under the iron law of the dictatorship of one party, has ended in a terrible fiasco. Russia teaches us how not to impose communism."

A pathetic appeal from the Russian anarcho-syndicalists to the world proletariat was published in the January 7–14, 1921, issue of the French journal *Le Libertaire*: "Comrades, put an end to the domination of your bourgeoisie just as we have done here. But do not repeat our errors; do not let state communism establish itself in your countries!" In 1920 the German anarchist, Rudolf Rocker, who later lived and died in the United States, wrote *Die Bankrotte des Russischen Staatskommunismus* (The Bankruptcy of State Communism), which appeared in 1921. This was the first analysis to be made of the degeneration of the Russian Revolution. In his view the famous "dictatorship of the proletariat" was not the expression of the will of a single class, but the dictatorship of a party pretending to speak in the name of a class and kept in power by force of bayonets. "Under the dictatorship of the proletariat in

Russia a new class has developed, the 'commissarocracy,' which oppresses the broad masses just as much as the old regime used to do." By systematically subordinating all the factors in social life to an all-powerful government endowed with every prerogative, "one could not fail to end up with the hierarchy of officials which proved fatal to the development of the Russian Revolution." "Not only did the Bolsheviks borrow the state apparatus from the previous society, but they have given it an all-embracing power which no other government arrogates to itself."

In June 1922 the group of Russian anarchists exiled in Germany published a revealing little book under the names of A. Gorielik, A. Komoff, and Voline: *Répression de l'Anarchisme en Russie Soviétique* (The Repression of Anarchism in Soviet Russia). Voline made a French translation which appeared at the beginning of 1923. It contained an alphabetical list of the martyrs of Russian anarchism. In 1921–1922, Alexander Berkman, and in 1922–1923, Emma Goldman published a succession of pamphlets on the dramatic events which they had witnessed in Russia.

In their turn, Peter Archinoff and Nestor Makhno himself, escaped Makhnovites who had taken refuge in the West, published their evidence.

The two great libertarian classics on the Russian Revolution, *The Guillotine at Work: Twenty Years of Terror in Russia* by G. P. Maximoff and *The Unkown Revolution* by Voline, came much later, during the Second World War, and were written with the maturity of thought made possible by the passage of the years.

For Maximoff, whose account appeared in America, the lessons of the past brought to him a sure expectation of a better future. The new ruling class in the U.S.S.R. cannot and will not be permanent, and it will be succeeded by libertarian socialism. Objective conditions are driving this development forward: "Is it conceivable . . . that the workers might desire the return of the capitalists to their enterprises? Never! for they are rebelling specifically against exploitation by the State and its bureaucrats." What the workers desire is to replace this authoritarian management of production with their own factory councils, and to unite these councils into one vast national federation. What they desire is workers' self-management. In the same way, the peasants have understood that there can be no question of returning to an individualist economy. Collective agriculture is the only solution, together with the collaboration of the rural collectives with the factory councils and trade unions: in short, the further development of the program of the October Revolution in complete freedom.

Voline strongly asserted that any experiment on the Russian model could only lead to "state capitalism based on an odious exploitation of the masses," the "worst form of capitalism and one which has absolutely nothing to do with the progress of humanity toward a socialist society." It could do nothing but promote "the dictatorship of a single party which leads unavoidably to the repression of all freedom of speech, press, organization, and action, even for revolutionary tendencies, with the sole exception of the party in power," and to a "social inquisition" which suffocates "the very breath of the Revolution." Voline went on to maintain that Stalin "did not fall from the moon." Stalin and Stalinism are, in his view, the logical consequence of the authoritarian system founded and established between 1918 and 1921. "This is the lesson the world must learn from the tremendous and decisive Bolshevik experiment: a lesson which gives powerful support to the libertarian thesis and which events will soon make clear to the understanding of all those who grieve, suffer, think, and struggle."

Anarchism in the Italian Factory Councils

The Italian anarchists followed the example of events in Russia, and went along with the partisans of soviet power in the period immediately after the Great War. The Russian Revolution had been received with deep sympathy by the Italian workers, especially by their vanguard, the metal workers of the northern part of the country. On February 20, 1919, the Italian Federation of Metal Workers (FIOM) won a contract providing for the election of "internal commissions" in the factories. They subsequently tried to transform these organs of workers' representation into factory councils with a managerial function, by conducting a series of strikes and occupations of the factories.

The last of these, at the end of August 1920, originated in a lockout by employers. The metal workers as a whole decided to continue production on their own. They tried persuasion and constraint alternately, but failed to win the cooperation of the engineers and supervisory personnel. The management of the factories had, therefore, to be conducted by technical and administrative workers' committees. Self-management went quite a long way: in the early period assistance was obtained from the banks, but when it was withdrawn the self-management system issued its own money to pay the workers' wages. Very strict self-discipline was required, the use of alcoholic beverages forbidden, and armed patrols were organized for self-defense. Very close solidarity was established between the factories under self-management. Ores and coal were put into a common pool, and shared out equitably.

The reformist wing of the trade unions opted for compromise with the employers. After a few weeks of managerial occupation, the workers had to leave the factories in exchange for a promise to extend workers' control, a promise which was not kept. The revolu-

109

tionary left wing, composed of anarchists and left socialists, cried treason, in vain.

This left wing had a theory, a spokesman, and a publication. The weekly *L'Ordine Nuovo* (The New Order) first appeared in Turin on May 1, 1919. It was edited by a left socialist, Antonio Gramsci, assisted by a professor of philosophy at Turin University with anarchist ideas, writing under the pseudonym of Carlo Petri, and also of a whole nucleus of Turin libertarians. In the factories, the *Ordine Nuovo* group was supported by a number of people, especially the anarcho-syndicalist militants of the metal trades, Pietro Ferrero and Maurizio Garino. The manifesto of *Ordine Nuovo* was signed by socialists and libertarians together, agreeing to regard the factory councils as "organs suited to future communist management of both the individual factory and the whole society."

Ordine Nuovo tended to replace traditional trade unionism by the structure of factory councils. It was not entirely hostile to trade unions, which it regarded as the "strong backbone of the great proletarian body." However, in the style of Malatesta in 1907, it was critical of the decadence of a bureaucratic and reformist trade-union movement, which had become an integral part of capitalist society; it denounced the inability of the trade unions to act as instruments of the proletarian revolution.

On the other hand, *Ordine Nuovo* attributed every virtue to the factory councils. It regarded them as the means of unifying the working class, the only organ which could raise the workers above the special interests of the different trades and link the "organized" with the "unorganized." It gave the councils credit for generating a producers' psychology, preparing the workers for self-management. Thanks to them the conquest of the factory became a concrete prospect for the lowliest worker, within his reach. The councils were regarded as a prefiguration of socialist society.

The Italian anarchists were of a more realistic and less verbose turn of mind than Antonio Gramsci, and sometimes indulged in ironic comment on the "thaumaturgical" excesses of the sermons in favor of factory councils. Of course they were aware of their merits, but stopped short of hyperbole. Gramsci denounced the reformism of the trade unions, not without reason, but the anarcho-syndicalists pointed out that in a nonrevolutionary period the factory councils, too, could degenerate into organs of class collaboration. Those most concerned with trade unionism also thought it unjust that *Ordine Nuovo* indiscriminately condemned not only reformist trade unionism but the revolutionary trade unionism of their center, the Italian Syndicalist Union.*

Lastly, and most important, the anarchists were somewhat uneasy about the ambiguous and contradictory interpretation which *Ordine Nuovo* put on the prototype of the factory councils, the soviets. Certainly Gramsci often used the term "libertarian" in his writings, and had crossed swords with the inveterate authoritarian Angelo Tasca, who propounded an undemocratic concept of the "dictatorship of the proletariat" which would reduce the factory councils to mere instruments of the Communist Party, and who even attacked Gramsci's thinking as "Proudhonian." Gramsci did not know enough about events in Russia to distinguish between the free soviets of the early months of the revolution and the tamed soviets of the Bolshevik State. This led him to use ambiguous formulations. He saw the factory council as the "model of the proletarian State," which he expected to be incorporated into a world system: the Communist International. He thought he could reconcile Bolshevism with the withering away of the State and a democratic interpretation of the "dictatorship of the proletariat."

The Italian anarchists had begun by welcoming the Russian soviets with uncritical enthusiasm. On June 1, 1919, Camillo Berneri, one of their number, had published an article entitled "Auto-Democracy" hailing the Bolshevik regime as "the most practical experiment in integral democracy on the largest scale yet attempted," and "the antithesis of centralizing state socialism."

---

* Debate among anarcho-syndicalists on the relative merits of factory councils and trade unions was, moreover, nothing new; it had recently divided the anarchists in Russia and even caused a split in the ranks of the editorial team in charge of the libertarian paper *Golos Truda*, some members remaining faithful to classical syndicalism while others, including G. P. Maximoff, opted for the councils.

However, a year later, at the congress of the Italian Anarchist Union, Maurizio Garino was talking quite differently: the soviets which had been set up in Russia by the Bolsheviks were materially different from workers' self-management as conceived by the anarchists. They formed the "basis of a new State, inevitably centralized and authoritarian."

The Italian anarchists and the friends of Gramsci were subsequently to follow divergent paths. The latter at first maintained that the Socialist Party, like the trade unions, was an organization integrated into the bourgeois system and that it was, consequently, neither necessary nor desirable to support it. They then made an "exception" for the communist groups within the Socialist Party. After the split at Livorno on January 21, 1921, these groups formed the Italian Communist Party, affiliated with the Communist International.

The Italian libertarians, for their part, had to abandon some of their illusions and pay more attention to a prophetic letter written to them by Malatesta as early as the summer of 1919. This warned them against "a new government which has set itself up [in Russia] above the Revolution in order to bridle it and subject it to the purposes of a particular party . . . or rather the leaders of a party." The old revolutionary argued prophetically that it was a dictatorship,

> with its decrees, its penal sanctions, its executive agents, and, above all, its armed forces which have served to defend the Revolution against its external enemies, but tomorrow will serve to impose the will of the dictators on the workers, to check the course of the Revolution, to consolidate newly established interests, and to defend a newly privileged class against the masses. Lenin, Trotsky, and their companions are certainly sincere revolutionaries, but they are preparing the governmental cadres which will enable their successors to profit by the Revolution and kill it. They will be the first victims of their own methods.

Two years later, the Italian Anarchist Union met in congress at Ancona on November 2–4, 1921, and refused to recognize the Russian government as a representative of the Revolution, instead denouncing it as "the main enemy of the Revolution," "the oppressor and exploiter of the proletariat in whose name it pretends to exercise authority." And the libertarian writer Luigi Fabbri in the same year concluded that "a critical study of the Russian Revolution is of immense importance . . . because the Western revolutionaries can direct their actions in such a way as to avoid the errors which have been brought to light by the Russian experience."

Anarchism in the Spanish Revolution

THE SOVIET MIRAGE

The time lag between subjective awareness and objective reality is a constant in history. The Russian anarchists and those who witnessed the Russian drama drew a lesson as early as 1920 which only became known, admitted, and shared years later. The first proletarian revolution in triumph over a sixth of the globe had such prestige and glitter that the working-class movement long remained hypnotized by so imposing an example. "Councils" in the image of the Russian soviets sprang up all over the place, not only in Italy, as we have seen, but in Germany, Austria, and Hungary. In Germany the system of councils was the essential item in the program of the Spartacus League of Rosa Luxemburg and Karl Liebknecht.

In 1919 the president of the Bavarian Republic, Kurt Eisner, was assassinated in Munich. A Soviet Republic was then proclaimed under the leadership of the libertarian writer Gustav Landauer, who was in turn assassinated by the counter-revolution. His friend and companion in arms, the anarchist poet Erich Mühsam, composed a *"Räte-Marseillaise"* (Marseillaise of the Councils), in which the workers were called to arms not to form battalions but councils on the model of those of Russia and Hungary, and thus to make an end of the centuries-old world of slavery.

However, in the spring of 1920 a German opposition group advocating *Räte-Kommunismus* (Communism of the councils) left the Communist Party to form a German Communist Workers

Party (KAPD).* The idea of councils inspired a similar group in Holland led by Hermann Gorter and Anton Pannekoek. During a lively polemic with Lenin, the former was not afraid to reply, in pure libertarian style, to the infallible leader of the Russian Revolution: "We are still looking for real leaders who will not seek to dominate the masses and will not betray them. As long as we do not have them we want everything to be done from the bottom upward and by the dictatorship of the masses over themselves. If I have a mountain guide and he leads me over a precipice, I prefer to do without." Pannekoek proclaimed that the councils were a form of self-government which would replace the forms of government of the old world; just like Gramsci he could see no difference between the latter and "Bolshevik dictatorship."

In many places, especially Bavaria, Germany, and Holland, the anarchists played a positive part in the practical and theoretical development of the system of councils.

Similarly, in Spain the anarcho-syndicalists were dazzled by the October Revolution. The Madrid congress of the CNT† (December 10–20, 1919), adopted a statement which stated that "the epic of the Russian people has electrified the world proletariat." By acclamation, "without reticence, as a beauty gives herself to the man she loves," the congress voted provisionally to join the Communist International because of its revolutionary character, expressing the hope, however, that a universal workers' congress would be called to determine the basis upon which a true workers' international could be built. A few timid voices of dissent were heard, however: the Russian Revolution was a "political" revolution and did not incorporate the libertarian ideal. The congress took no notice and decided to send a delegation to the Second Congress of the Third International which opened in Moscow on July 15, 1920.

By then, however, the love match was already on the way to breaking up. The delegate representing Spanish anarcho-syndicalism was pressed to take part in establishing an international revolu-

---

* In April 1922, the KAPD set up a "Communist Workers International" with Dutch and Belgian opposition groups.

† The Spanish National Confederation of Labor.

tionary trade-union center, but he jibed when presented with a text which referred to the "conquest of political power," "the dictatorship of the proletariat," and proposed an organic relationship between the trade unions and the communist parties which thinly disguised a relationship of subordination of the former to the latter. In the forthcoming meetings of the Communist International the trade-union organizations of the different nations would be represented by the delegates of the communist parties of their respective countries; and the projected Red Trade-Union International would be openly controlled by the Communist International and its national sections. Angel Pestaña, the Spanish spokesman, set forth the libertarian conception of the social revolution and exclaimed: "The revolution is not, and cannot be, the work of a party. The most a party can do is to foment a *coup d'état*. But a *coup d'état* is not a revolution." He concluded: "You tell us that the revolution cannot take place without a communist party and that without the conquest of political power emancipation is not possible, and that without dictatorship one cannot destroy the bourgeoisie: all these assertions are absolutely gratuitous."

In view of the doubts expressed by the CNT delegate, the communists made a show of adjusting the resolution with regard to the "dictatorship of the proletariat." The Russian trade-union leader Lozovsky nevertheless ultimately published the text in its original form without the modifications introduced by Pestaña, but bearing his signature. From the rostrum Trotsky had laid into the Spanish delegate for nearly an hour but the president declared the debate closed when Pestaña asked for time to reply to these attacks.

Pestaña spent several months in Moscow and left Russia on September 6, 1920, profoundly disillusioned by all that he had observed during that time. In an account of a subsequent visit to Berlin, Rudolf Rocker described Pestaña as being like a man "saved from a shipwreck." He had not the heart to tell his Spanish comrades the truth. It seemed to him like "murder" to destroy the immense hope which the Russian Revolution had raised in them. As soon as he crossed the Spanish border he was thrown into prison and was thus spared the painful duty of being the first to speak.

During the summer of 1921 a different delegation from the CNT took part in the founding congress of the Red Trade-Union International. Among the CNT delegates there were young disciples of Russian Bolshevism, such as Joaquín Maurin and Andrés Nin, but there was also a French anarchist, Gaston Leval, who had a cool head. He took the risk of being accused of "playing the game of the bourgeoisie" and "helping the counter-revolution" rather than keep silent. Not to tell the masses that what had failed in Russia was not the Revolution, but the State, and not "to show them behind the living Revolution, the State which was paralyzing and killing it," would have been worse than silence. He used these terms, in *Le Libertaire* in November 1921. He thought that "any honest and loyal collaboration" with the Bolsheviks had become impossible and, on his return to Spain, recommended to the CNT that it withdraw from the Third International and its bogus trade-union affiliate.

Having been given this lead, Pestaña decided to publish his first report and, subsequently, extend it by a second in which he would reveal the entire truth about Bolshevism:

> The principles of the Communist Party are exactly the opposite of those which it was affirming and proclaiming during the first hours of the Revolution. The principles, methods, and final objectives of the Communist Party are diametrically opposed to those of the Russian Revolution . . . . As soon as the Communist Party had obtained absolute power, it decreed that anyone who did not think as a communist (that is, according to its own definition) had no right to think at all . . . . The Communist Party has denied to the Russian proletariat all the sacred rights which the Revolution had conferred upon it.

Pestaña, further, cast doubt on the validity of the Communist International: a simple extension of the Russian Communist Party, it could not represent the Revolution in the eyes of the world proletariat.

The national congress of the CNT held at Saragossa in June 1922 received this report and decided to withdraw from the trade-union front, the Red Trade-Union International. It was also decided to send delegates to an international anarcho-syndicalist conference held in Berlin in December, from which resulted a

"Workers' International Association." This was not a real international, since aside from the important Spanish group, it had the support of very small numbers in other countries.*

From the time of this breach Moscow bore an inveterate hatred for Spanish anarchism. Joaquín Maurin and Andrés Nin were disowned by the CNT and left it to found the Spanish Communist Party. In May 1924 Maurin published a pamphlet declaring war to the death on his former comrades: "The complete elimination of anarchism is a difficult task in a country in which the workers' movement bears the mark of fifty years of anarchist propaganda. *But we shall get them.*" A threat which was later carried out.

THE ANARCHIST TRADITION
IN SPAIN

The Spanish anarchists had thus learned the lesson of the Russian Revolution very early, and this played a part in inspiring them to prepare an antinomian revolution. The degeneration of authoritarian communism increased their determination to bring about the victory of a libertarian form of communism. They had been cruelly disappointed in the Soviet mirage and, in the words of Diego Abad de Santillan, saw in anarchism "the last hope of renewal during this somber period."

The basis for a libertarian revolution was pretty well laid in the consciousness of the popular masses and in the thinking of libertarian theoreticians. According to José Peirats, anarcho-syndicalism was, "because of its psychology, its temperament, and its reactions, the most Spanish thing in all Spain." It was the double product of a compound development. It suited both the backward state of a poorly developed country, in which rural living conditions remained archaic, and also the growth of a modern prole-

---

* In France, for example, the trade unionists who followed Pierre Besnard were expelled from the Conféderation Générale du Travail Unitaire (obedient to the Communists) and, in 1924, founded the Confédération Générale du Travail Syndicaliste Révolutionnaire.

tariat born of industrialization in certain areas. The unique feature of Spanish anarchism was a strange mixture of past and future. The symbiosis between these two tendencies was far from perfect. In 1918, the CNT had more than a million trade-union members.

In the industrial field it was strong in Catalonia, and rather less so in Madrid and Valencia;* but it also had deep roots in the countryside, among the poor peasants who preserved a tradition of village communalism, tinged with local patriotism and a cooperative spirit. In 1898 the author Joaquín Costa had described the survivals of this agrarian collectivism. Many villages still had common property from which they allocated plots to the landless, or which they used together with other villages for pasturage or other communal purposes. In the region of large-scale landowner-ship, in the south, the agricultural day laborers preferred socialization to the division of the land.

Moreover, many decades of anarchist propaganda in the countryside, in the form of small popular pamphlets, had prepared the basis for agrarian collectivism. The CNT was especially powerful among the peasants of the south (Andalusia), of the east (area of the Levant around Valencia), and of the northeast (Aragon, around Saragossa).

This double base, both industrial and rural, had turned the libertarian communism of Spanish anarcho-syndicalism in somewhat divergent directions, the one communalist, the other syndicalist. The communalism was expressed in a more local, more rural spirit, one might almost say: more southern, for one of its principal bastions was in Andalusia. Syndicalism, on the other hand, was more urban and unitarian in spirit—more northerly, too, since its main center was Catalonia. Libertarian theoreticians were somewhat torn and divided on this subject.

Some had given their hearts to Kropotkin and his erudite but simplistic idealization of the communes of the Middle Ages which they identified with the Spanish tradition of the primitive peasant community. Their favorite slogan was the "free commune." Vari-

* Whereas in Castile and in the Asturias, etc., the social-democratic trade-union center, the General Union of Workers (UGT) was predominant.

ous practical experiments in libertarian communism took place during the peasant insurrections which followed the foundation of the Republic in 1931. By free mutual agreement some groups of small-peasant proprietors decided to work together, to divide the profits into equal parts, and to provide for their own consumption by "drawing from the common pool." They dismissed the municipal administrations and replaced them by elected committees, naïvely believing that they could free themselves from the surrounding society, taxation, and military service.

Bakunin was the founder of the Spanish collectivist, syndicalist, and internationalist workers' movement. Those anarchists who were more realistic, more concerned with the present than the golden age, tended to follow him and his disciple Ricardo Mella. They were concerned with economic unification and believed that a long transitional period would be necessary during which it would be wiser to reward labor according to the hours worked and not according to need. They envisaged the economic structure of the future as a combination of local trade-union groupings and federations of branches of industry.

For a long time the *sindicatos únicos* (local unions) predominated within the CNT. These groups, close to the workers, free from all corporate egoism, served as a physical and spiritual home for the proletariat.* Training in these local unions had fused the ideas of the trade union and the commune in the minds of rank-and-file militants.

The theoretical debate in which the syndicalists opposed the anarchists at the International Anarchist Congress of 1907† was revived in practice to divide the Spanish anarcho-syndicalists. The struggle for day-to-day demands within the CNT had created a reformist tendency in the face of which the FAI (Federación Anarquista Ibérica), founded in 1927, undertook the defense of

---

* The CNT only agreed to the creation of industrial federations in 1931. In 1919 this had been rejected by the "pure" anarchists as leading toward centralism and bureaucracy; but it had become essential to reply to the concentration of capitalism by the concentration of the unions in a single industry. The large industrial federations were only really stabilized in 1937.

† See pages 78–80.

the integrity of anarchist doctrines. In 1931 a "Manifesto of the Thirty" was put out by the syndicalist tendency condemning the "dictatorship" of minorities within the trade-union movement, and declaring the independence of trade unionism and its claim to be sufficient unto itself. Some trade unions left the CNT and a reformist element persisted within that trade-union center even after the breach had been healed on the eve of the July 1936 Revolution.

THEORY

The Spanish anarchists continuously published the major and even minor works of international anarchism in the Spanish language. They thus preserved from neglect, and even perhaps absolute destruction, the traditions of a socialism both revolutionary and free. Augustin Souchy was a German anarcho-syndicalist writer who put himself at the service of Spanish anarchism. According to him, "the problem of the social revolution was continuously and systematically discussed in their trade-union and group meetings, in their papers, their pamphlets, and their books."

The proclamation of the Spanish Republic, in 1931, led to an outburst of "anticipatory" writings: Peirats lists about fifty titles, stressing that there were many more, and emphasizes that this "obsession with revolutionary construction" led to a proliferation of writings which contributed greatly to preparing the people for a revolutionary road. James Guillaume's pamphlet of 1876, *Idées sur l'Organisation Sociale*, was known to the Spanish anarchists because it had been largely quoted in Pierre Besnard's book, *Les Syndicats Ouvriers et la Révolution Sociale*, which appeared in Paris in 1930. Gaston Leval had emigrated to the Argentine and in 1931 published *Social Reconstruction in Spain*, which gave direct inspiration to the important work of Diego Abad de Santillan, to be discussed below.

In 1932, the country doctor Isaac Puente published a rather naïve and idealistic outline of libertarian communism; its ideas were taken up by the Saragossa congress of the CNT in May 1936. Puente himself had become the moving spirit of an insurrectionary committee in Aragon in 1933.

The Saragossa program of 1936 defined the operation of a direct village democracy with some precision. A communal council was to be elected by a general assembly of the inhabitants and formed of representatives of various technical committees. The general assembly was to meet whenever the interests of the commune required it, on the request of members of the communal council or on the direct demand of the inhabitants. The various responsible positions would have no executive or bureaucratic character. The incumbents (with the exception of a few technicians and statisticians) would carry out their duties as producers, like everybody else, meeting at the end of the day's work to discuss matters of detail which did not require decisions by the general assembly.

Active workers were to receive a producer's card on which would be recorded the amount of labor performed, evaluated in daily units, which could be exchanged for goods. The inactive members of the population would receive simply a consumer's card. There was to be no general norm: the autonomy of the communes was to be respected. If they thought fit, they could establish a different system of internal exchange, on the sole condition that it did not injure the interests of the other communes. The right to communal autonomy would, however, not obviate the duty of collective solidarity within the provincial and regional federations of communes.

One of the major concerns of the members of the Saragossa congress was the cultivation of the mind. Throughout their lives all men were to be assured of access to science, art, and research of all kinds, provided only that these activities remained compatible with production of material resources. Society was no longer to be divided into manual workers and intellectuals: all were to be, simultaneously, both one and the other. The practice of such parallel activities would insure a healthy balance in human nature. Once his day's work as a producer was finished the individual was to be the absolute master of his own time. The CNT foresaw that spiritual needs would begin to be expressed in a far more pressing way as soon as the emancipated society had satis-fied material needs.

Spanish anarcho-syndicalism had long been concerned to safe-guard the autonomy of what it called "affinity groups." There were many adepts of naturism and vegetarianism among its members, especially among the poor peasants of the south. Both these ways of living were considered suitable for the transformation of the human being in preparation for a libertarian society. At the Saragossa congress the members did not forget to consider the fate of groups of naturists and nudists, "unsuited to industrialization." As these groups would be unable to supply all their own needs, the congress anticipated that their delegates to the meetings of the confederation of communes would be able to negotiate special economic agreements with the other agricultural and industrial communes. Does this make us smile? On the eve of a vast, bloody, social transformation, the CNT did not think it foolish to try to meet the infinitely varied aspirations of individual human beings.

With regard to crime and punishment the Saragossa congress followed the teachings of Bakunin, stating that social injustice is the main cause of crime and, consequently, once this has been removed offenses will rarely be committed. The congress affirmed that man is not naturally evil. The shortcomings of the individual, in the moral field as well as in his role as producer, were to be in-vestigated by popular assemblies which would make every effort to find a just solution in each separate case.

Libertarian communism was unwilling to recognize the need for any penal methods other than medical treatment and re-education. If, as the result of some pathological condition, an indi-vidual were to damage the harmony which should reign among his equals he would be treated for his unbalanced condition, at the same time that his ethical and social sense would be stimu-lated. If erotic passions were to go beyond the bounds imposed by respect for the freedom of others, the Saragossa congress recom-mended a "change of air," believing it to be as good for physical illness as for lovesickness. The trade-union federation really doubted that such extreme behavior would still occur in surroundings of sexual freedom.

When the CNT congress adopted the Saragossa program in May 1936, no one really expected that the time to apply it would come only two months later. In practice the socialization of the land and of industry which was to follow the revolutionary victory of July 19 differed considerably from this idyllic program. While the word "commune" occurred in every line, the term actually used for socialist production units was to be *collectividades*. This was not simply a change of terminology: the creators of Spanish self-management looked to other sources for their inspiration.

Two months before the Saragossa congress Diego Abad de Santillan had published a book, *El Organismo Económico de la Revolución* (The Economic Organization of the Revolution). This outline of an economic structure drew a somewhat different inspiration from the Saragossa program.

Unlike many of his contemporaries, Santillan was not a rigid and sterile disciple of the great anarchists of the nineteenth century. He regretted that anarchist literature of the previous twenty-five or thirty years should have paid so little attention to the concrete problems of a new economy, and that it had not opened up original perspectives on the future. On the other hand, anarchism had produced a superabundance of works, in every language, going over and over an entirely abstract conception of liberty. Santillan compared this indigestible body of work with the reports presented to the national and international congresses of the First International, and the latter seemed to him the more brilliant for the comparison. He thought they had shown a very much better understanding of economic problems than had appeared in subsequent periods.

Santillan was not backward, but a true man of his times. He was aware that "the tremendous development of modern industry has created a whole series of new problems, which it was impossible to foresee at an earlier time." There is no question of going back to the Roman chariot or to primitive forms of artisan production. Economic insularity, a parochial way of thinking, the *patria chica* (little fatherland) dear to the hearts of rural Spaniards nostalgic for a golden age, the small-scale and medieval "free commune" of Kropotkin—all these must be relegated to a museum of antiquities. They are the vestiges of out-of-date communalist con-

ceptions. No "free communes" can exist from the economic point
of view: "Our ideal is the commune which is associated, federated,
integrated into the total economy of the country, and of other
countries in a state of revolution." To replace the single owner
by a hydra-headed owner is not collectivism, is not self-management. The land, the factories, the mines, the means of transport
are the product of the work of all and must be at the service of
all. Nowadays the economy is neither local, nor even national, but
world-wide. The characteristic feature of modern life is the cohesion of all the productive and distributive forces. "A socialized
economy, directed and planned, is an imperative necessity and
corresponds to the trend of development of the modern economic
world."

Santillan foresaw the function of coordinating and planning as
being carried out by a federal economic council, which would
not be a political authority, but simply an organ of coordination,
an economic and administrative regulator. Its directives would
come from below, from the factory councils federated into trade-
union councils for different branches of industry, and into local
economic councils. The federal council is thus at the receiving
end of two chains of authority, one based on locality and the
other on occupation. The organizations at the base provide it
with statistics so that it will be aware of the real economic situation at any given moment. In this way it can spot major deficien-
cies, and determine the sectors in which new industries or crops
are most urgently required. "The policemen will no longer be
necessary when the supreme authority lies in figures and statistics."
In such a system state coercion has no utility, is sterile, even impossible. The federal council sees to the propagation of new
norms, the growth of interdependence between the regions and
the formation of national solidarity. It stimulates research into
new methods of work, new manufacturing processes, new agricultural techniques. It distributes labor from one region to another, from one branch of the economy to another.

There is no doubt that Santillan learned a great deal from the
Russian Revolution. On the one hand, it taught him to beware of
the danger of a resurgence of the state and bureaucratic apparatus;
but, on the other, it taught him that a victorious revolution can-

not avoid passing through intermediate economic forms,* in which there survives for a time what Marx and Lenin call "bourgeois law." For instance, there could be no question of abolishing the banking and monetary system at one fell swoop. These institutions must be transformed and used as a temporary means of exchange to keep social life moving and prepare the way to new economic forms.

Santillan was to play an important part in the Spanish Revolution: he became, in turn, a member of the central committee of the anti-fascist militia (end of July 1936), a member of the Catalonian Economic Council (August 11), and Economics Minister of the Catalonian government (mid-December).

AN "APOLITICAL" REVOLUTION

The Spanish Revolution was, thus, relatively well prepared, both in the minds of libertarian thinkers and in the consciousness of the people. It is therefore not surprising that the Spanish Right regarded the electoral victory of the Popular Front in February 1936 as the beginning of a revolution.

In fact, the masses soon broke out of the narrow framework of their success at the ballot box. They ignored the rules of the parliamentary game and did not even wait for a government to be formed to set the prisoners free. The farmers ceased to pay rent to the landlords, the agricultural day laborers occupied land and began to cultivate it, the villagers got rid of their municipal councils and hastened to administer themselves, the railwaymen went on strike to enforce a demand for the nationalization of the railways. The building workers of Madrid called for workers' control, the first step toward socialization.

The military chiefs, under the leadership of Colonel Franco, responded to the symptoms of revolution by a *putsch*. But they only succeeded in accelerating the progress of a revolution which

---

* Not to be confused with intermediate *political* forms, which the anarchists, unlike the Marxists, reject.

had, in fact, already begun. In Madrid, in Barcelona, in Valencia particularly, in almost every big city but Seville, the people took the offensive, besieged barracks, set up barricades in the streets and occupied strategic positions. The workers rushed from all sides to answer the call of their trade unions. They assaulted the strongholds of the Franco forces, with no concern for their own lives, with naked hands and uncovered breasts. They succeeded in taking guns from the enemy and persuading soldiers to join their ranks.

Thanks to this popular fury the military *putsch* was checked within the first twenty-four hours; and then the social revolution began quite spontaneously. It went forward unevenly, of course, in different regions and cities, but with the greatest impetuosity in Catalonia and, especially, Barcelona. When the established authorities recovered from their astonishment, they found that they simply no longer existed. The State, the police, the army, the administration, all seemed to have lost their *raison d'être*. The Civil Guard had been driven off or liquidated and the victorious workers were maintaining order. The most urgent task was to organize food supplies: committees distributed foodstuffs from barricades transformed into canteens, and then opened communal restaurants. Local administration was organized by neighborhood committees, and war committees saw to the departure of the workers' militia to the front. The trade-union center had become the real town hall. This was no longer the "defense of the republic" against fascism, it was the Revolution—a Revolution which, unlike the Russian one, did not have to create all its organs of authority from scratch: the election of soviets was made unnecessary by the omnipresent anarcho-syndicalist organization with its various committees at the base. In Catalonia the CNT and its conscious minority, the FAI, were more powerful than the authorities, which had become mere phantoms.

In Barcelona especially, there was nothing to prevent the workers' committees from seizing *de jure* the power which they were already exercising *de facto*. But they did not do so. For decades, Spanish anarchism had been warning the people against the deceptions of "politics" and emphasizing the primacy of the "economic." It had constantly sought to divert the people from a bourgeois democratic revolution in order to lead them to the social revolution through direct action. On the brink of the Revolution, the anarchists argued something like this: let the politicians do what they will; we, the "apolitical," will lay hands on the economy. On September 3, 1936, the *CNT-FAI Information Bulletin* published an article entitled "The Futility of Government," suggesting that the economic expropriation which was taking place would lead *ipso facto* to the "liquidation of the bourgeois State, which would die of asphyxiation."

ANARCHISTS IN GOVERNMENT

This underestimation of government, however, was very rapidly reversed and the Spanish anarchists suddenly became governmentalists. Soon after the Revolution of July 19 in Barcelona, an interview took place between the anarchist activist García Oliver and the president of the Catalonian government, the bourgeois liberal Companys. He was ready to resign but was kept in office. The CNT and the FAI refused to exercise an anarchist "dictatorship," and declared their willingness to collaborate with other left groupings. By mid-September, the CNT was calling on the prime minister of the central government, Largo Caballero, to set up a fifteen-member "Defense Council" in which they would be satisfied with five places. This was as good as accepting the idea of participating in a cabinet under another name.

The anarchists ended up by accepting portfolios in two governments: first in Catalonia and subsequently in Madrid. The Italian anarchist, Camillo Berneri, was in Barcelona and, on April 14, 1937, wrote an open letter to his comrade, minister Federica Montseny, reproaching the anarchists with being in the government only as hostages and fronts "for politicians who flirt with the [class] enemy." * It is true that the State with which the

---

* The International Workers' Association to which the CNT was affiliated held a special congress in Paris, June 11–13, 1937, at which the anarcho-syndicalist trade-union center was reproached for participating in government and for the concessions it had made in consequence. With this back-

Spanish anarchists had agreed to become integrated remained a bourgeois State whose officials and political personnel often had but little loyalty to the republic. What was the reason for this change of heart?

The Spanish Revolution had taken place as the consequence of a proletarian counterattack against a counter-revolutionary *coup d'état*. From the beginning the Revolution took on the character of self-defense, a military character, because of the necessity to oppose the cohorts of Colonel Franco with anti-fascist militia. Faced by a common danger, the anarchists thought that they had no choice but to join with all the other trade-union forces, and even political parties, which were ready to stand against the Franco rebellion. As the fascist powers increased their support for Franco, the anti-fascist struggle degenerated into a real war, a total war of the classical type. The libertarians could only take part in it by abandoning more and more of their principles, both political and military. They reasoned, falsely, that the victory of the Revolution could only be assured by first winning the war and, as Santillan was to admit, they "sacrificed everything" to the war. Berneri argued in vain against the priority of the war as such, and maintained that the defeat of Franco could only be insured by a *revolutionary* war. To put a brake on the Revolution was, in fact, to weaken the strongest arm of the Republic: the active participation of the masses. An even more serious aspect of the matter was that Republican Spain, blockaded by the Western democracies and in grave danger from the advancing fascist troups, needed Russian military aid in order to survive. This aid was given on a two-fold condition: 1) the Communist Party must profit from it as much as possible, and the anarchists as little as possible; 2) Stalin wanted at any price to prevent the victory of a social revolution in Spain, not only because it would have been libertarian, but because it would have expropriated capital investments belonging to Britain which was presumed to

---

ing, Sébastien Faure decided to publish a series of articles in the July 8, 15, and 22 issues of *Le Libertaire*, entitled "The Fatal Slope." These were severely critical of the decision of the Spanish anarchists to take part in government. The CNT was enraged and brought about the resignation of the secretary of the International Workers' Association, Pierre Besnard.

be an ally of the U.S.S.R. in the "democratic alliance" against Hitler. The Spanish Communists went so far as to deny that a revolution had taken place: a legal government was simply trying to overcome a military mutiny. In May 1937, there was a bloody struggle in Barcelona and the workers were disarmed by the forces of order under Stalinist command. In the name of united action against the fascists the anarchists forbade the workers to retaliate. The sad persistence with which they threw themselves into the error of the Popular Front, until the final defeat of the Republic, cannot be dealt with in this short book.

SELF-MANAGEMENT IN AGRICULTURE

Nevertheless, in the field to which they attached the greatest importance, the economic field, the Spanish anarchists showed themselves much more intransigent and compromised to a much lesser degree. Agricultural and industrial self-management was very largely self-propelled. But as the State grew stronger and the war more and more totalitarian, an increasingly sharp contradiction developed between a bourgeois republic at war and an experiment in communism or rather in libertarian collectivism. In the end, it was self-management which had to retreat, sacrificed on the altar of "antifascism." According to Peirats, a methodical study of this experiment in self-management has yet to be made; it will be a difficult task, since self-management presented so many variants in different places and at different times. This matter deserves all the more attention, because relatively little is known about it. Even within the Republican ranks it was either passed over or under-rated. The civil war submerged it and even today overshadows it in human memory. For example, there is no reference to it in the film *To Die in Madrid*, and yet it is probably the most creative legacy of Spanish anarchism.

The Revolution of July 19, 1936, was a lightning defensive action by the people to counter the *pronunciamento* of Franco. The industrialists and large landowners immediately abandoned their property and took refuge abroad. The workers and peasants took over this abandoned property, the agricultural day laborers decided to continue cultivating the soil on their own. They associated together in "collectives" quite spontaneously. In Catalonia a regional congress of peasants was called together by the CNT on September 5 and agreed to the collectivization of land under trade-union management and control. Large estates and the property of fascists were to be socialized, while small landowners would have free choice between individual property and collective property. Legal sanction came later: on October 7, 1936, the Republican central government confiscated without indemnity the property of "persons compromised in the fascist rebellion." This measure was incomplete from a legal point of view, since it only sanctioned a very small part of the take-overs already carried out spontaneously by the people; the peasants had carried out expropriation without distinguishing between those who had taken part in the military *putsch* and those who had not.

In underdeveloped countries where the technical resources necessary for large-scale agriculture are absent, the poor peasant is more attracted by private property, which he has not yet enjoyed, than by socialized agiculture. In Spain, however, libertarian education and a collectivist tradition compensated for technical underdevelopment, countered the individualistic tendencies of the peasants, and turned them directly toward socialism. The latter was the choice of the poorer peasants, while those who were slightly better off, as in Catalonia, clung to individualism. A great majority (90 percent) of land workers chose to join collectives from the very beginning. This decision created a close alliance between the peasants and the city workers, the latter being supporters of the socialization of the means of production by the very nature of their function. It seems that social consciousness was even higher in the country than in the cities.

The agricultural collectives set themselves up with a twofold management, economic and geographical. The two functions were distinct, but in most cases it was the trade unions which assumed them or controlled them. A general assembly of working peasants in each village elected a management committee which was to be responsible for economic administration. Apart from the secretary, all the members continued their manual labor. Work was obligatory for all healthy men between eighteen and sixty. The peasants were divided into groups of ten or more, each led by a delegate, and each being allocated an area to cultivate, or an operation to perform, appropriate to the age of its members and the nature of the work concerned. The management committee received the delegates from the groups every evening. With regard to local administration, the commune frequently called the inhabitants together in general assembly to receive reports of activities undertaken. Everything was put into the common pool with the exception of clothing, furniture, personal savings, small domestic animals, garden plots, and poultry kept for family use. Artisans, hairdressers, shoemakers, etc., were grouped in collectives; the sheep belonging to the community were divided into flocks of several hundreds, put in the charge of shepherds, and methodically distributed in the mountain pastures.

With regard to the distribution of products, various systems were tried out, some based on collectivism and others on more or less total communism, and still others resulting from a combination of the two. Most commonly, payment was based on family needs. Each head of a family received a daily wage of specially marked pesetas which could only be exchanged for consumer goods in the communal shops, which were often set up in the church or its buildings. Any balance not consumed was placed in a peseta credit account for the benefit of the individual. It was possible to draw a limited amount of pocket money from this balance. Rent, electricity, medical care, pharmaceuticals, old-age assistance, etc., were all free. Education was also free and often given in schools set up in former convents; it was compulsory for all children under fourteen, who were forbidden to perform manual labor.

Membership in the collective continued to be voluntary, as was required by the basic concern of the anarchist for freedom. No pressure was brought to bear on the small farmers. Choosing to remain outside the community, they could not expect to receive its services and benefits since they claimed to be sufficient unto themselves. However, they could opt to participate as they wished in communal work and they could bring their produce to the communal shops. They were admitted to general assemblies and the enjoyment of some collective benefits. They were forbidden only to take over more land than they could cultivate, and subject to only one restriction: that their presence or their property should not disturb the socialist order. In some places socialized areas were reconstituted into larger units by voluntary exchange of plots with individual peasants. In most villages individualists, whether peasants or traders, decreased in number as time went on. They felt isolated and preferred to join the collectives.

It appears that the units which applied the collectivist principle of day wages were more solid than the comparatively few which tried to establish complete communism too quickly, taking no account of the egoism still deeply rooted in human nature, especially among the women. In some villages where currency had been suppressed and the population helped itself from the common pool, producing and consuming within the narrow limits of the collectives, the disadvantages of this paralyzing self-sufficiency made themselves felt, and individualism soon returned to the fore, causing the breakup of the community by the withdrawal of many former small farmers who had joined but did not have a really communist way of thinking.

The communes were united into cantonal federations, above which were regional federations. In theory all the lands belonging to a cantonal federation were treated as a single unit without intermediate boundaries.* Solidarity between villages was pushed to the limit, and equalization funds made it possible to give assistance to the poorest collectives. Tools, raw materials, and surplus labor were all made available to communities in need.

The extent of rural socialization was different in different provinces. As already said, Catalonia was an area of small- and medium-sized farms, and the peasantry had a strong individualistic tradition, so that here there were no more than a few pilot collectives. In Aragon, on the other hand, more than three-quarters of the land was socialized. The creative initiative of the agricultural workers in this region had been stimulated by a libertarian militia

---

* "In theory," because there was some litigation between villages on this subject.

unit, the Durruti Column, passing through on its way to the northern front to fight the Franco troops, and by the subsequent establishment of a revolutionary authority created at the base, which was unique of its kind in Republican Spain. About 450 collectives were set up, with some half a million members. In the Levant region (five provinces, capital Valencia), the richest in Spain, some 900 collectives were established, covering 43 percent of the geographical area, 50 percent of citrus production, and 70 percent of the citrus trade. In Castile, about 300 collectives were created, with around 100,000 members. Socialization also made headway in Estremadura and part of Andalusia, while a few early attempts were quickly repressed in the Asturias.

It should be remembered that grass-roots socialism was not the work of the anarcho-syndicalists alone, as many people have supposed. According to Gaston Leval, the supporters of self-management were often "libertarians without knowing it." In Estremadura and Andalusia, the social-democratic, Catholic, and in the Asturias even communist, peasants took the initiative in collectivization. However, in the southern areas not controlled by the anarchists, where municipalities took over large estates in an authoritarian manner, the day laborers unfortunately did not feel this to be a revolutionary transformation: their wages and conditions were not changed; there was no self-management.

Agricultural self-management was an indisputable success except where it was sabotaged by its opponents or interrupted by the war. It was not difficult to beat the record of large-scale private ownership, for it had been deplorable. Some 10,000 feudal landowners had been in possession of half the territory of the Spanish Peninsula. It had suited them to let a large part of their land lie fallow rather than to permit the development of a stratum of independent farmers, or to give their day laborers decent wages; to do either of these would have undermined their medieval feudal authority. Thus their existence had retarded the full development of the natural wealth of the Spanish land.

After the Revolution the land was brought together into rational units, cultivated on a large scale and according to the general plan and directives of agronomists. The studies of agricultural technicians brought about yields 30 to 50 percent higher than

before. The cultivated areas increased, human, animal, and mechanical energy was used in a more rational way, and working
methods perfected. Crops were diversified, irrigation extended, re-
forestation initiated, and tree nurseries started. Piggeries were
constructed, rural technical schools built, and demonstration
farms set up, selective cattle breeding was developed, and aux-
iliary agricultural industries put into operation. Socialized agriculture showed itself superior on the one hand to large-scale
absentee ownership, which left part of the land fallow; and on
the other to small farms cultivated by primitive techniques, with
poor seed and no fertilizers.

A first attempt at agricultural planning was made, based on
production and consumption statistics produced by the collectives,
brought together by the respective cantonal committees and then
by the regional committee which controlled the quantity and
quality of production within its area. Trade outside the region
was handled by a regional committee which collected the goods
to be sold and in exchange for them bought the goods required
by the region as a whole. Rural anarcho-syndicalism showed its
organizational ability and capacity for coordination to best advantage in the Levant. The export of citrus required methodical
modern commercial techniques; they were brilliantly put into play,
in spite of a few lively disputes with rich producers.

Cultural development went hand in hand with material pros-
perity: a campaign was undertaken to bring literacy to adults;
regional federations set up a program of lectures, films, and
theatrical performances in all the villages. These successes were
due not only to the strength of the trade-union organization but,
to a considerable degree, also to the intelligence and initiative
of the people. Although the majority of them were illiterate, the
peasants showed a degree of socialist consciousness, practical good
sense, and spirit of solidarity and sacrifice which drew the admiration of foreign observers. Fenner Brockway, then of the
British Independent Labour Party, now Lord Brockway, visited
the collective of Segorbe and reported: "The spirit of the peasants, their enthusiasm, and the way they contribute to the common effort and the pride which they take in it, are all admirable."

SELF-MANAGEMENT IN INDUSTRY

Self-management was also tried out in industry, especially in Catalonia, the most industrialized area in Spain. Workers whose employers had fled spontaneously undertook to keep the factories going. For more than four months, the factories of Barcelona, over which waved the red and black flag of the CNT, were managed by revolutionary workers' committees without help or interference from the State, sometimes even without experienced managerial help. The proletariat had one piece of good fortune in being aided by technicians. In Russia in 1917–1918, and in Italy in 1920, during those brief experiments in the occupation of the factories, the engineers had refused to help the new experiment of socialization; in Spain many of them collaborated closely with the workers from the very beginning.

A trade-union conference representing 600,000 workers was held in Barcelona in October 1936, with the object of developing the socialization of industry. The initiative of the workers was institutionalized by a decree of the Catalan government dated October 24, 1936. This ratified the *fait accompli*, but introduced an element of government control alongside self-management. Two sectors were created, one socialist, the other private. All factories with more than a hundred workers were to be socialized (and those with between fifty and a hundred could be, on the request of three-quarters of the workers), as were those whose proprietors either had been declared "subversive" by a people's court or had stopped production, and those whose importance justified taking them out of the private sector. (In fact many enterprises were socialized because they were heavily in debt.)

A factory under self-management was directed by a managerial committee of five to fifteen members representing the various trades and services. They were nominated by the workers in general assembly and served for two years, half being changed each year. The committee appointed a manager to whom it delegated all or part of its own powers. In very large factories the selection of a manager required the approval of the supervisory organization. Moreover, a government controller was appointed to each management committee. In effect it was not complete self-management but a sort of joint management in very close liaison with the Catalonian government.

The management committee could be recalled, either by the general meeting of the workers or by the general council of the particular branch of the industry (composed of four representatives of management committees, eight of the trade unions, and four technicians appointed by the supervisory organization). This general council planned the work and determined the division of the profits, and its decisions were mandatory. In those enterprises which remained in private hands an elected workers' committee was to control the production process and conditions of work "in close collaboration with the employer." The wage system was maintained intact in the socialized factories. Each worker continued to be paid a fixed wage. Profits were not divided on the factory level and wages rose very little after socialization, in fact even less than in the sector which remained private.

The decree of October 24, 1936, was a compromise between aspirations to self-management and the tendency to tutelage by the leftist government, as well as a compromise between capitalism and socialism. It was drafted by a libertarian minister, and ratified by the CNT, because anarchist leaders were in the government. How could they object to the intervention of government in self-management when they themselves had their hands on the levers of power? Once the wolf is allowed into the sheepfold he always ends up by acting as its master.

In spite of the considerable powers which had been given to the general councils of branches of industry, it appeared in practice that workers' self-management tended to produce a sort of parochial egoism, a species of "bourgeois cooperativism," as Peirats called it, each production unit concerning itself only with its own interests. There were rich collectives and poor collectives. Some could pay relatively high wages while others could not even manage to maintain the wage level which had prevailed before the Revolution. Some had plenty of raw materials, others were very short, etc. This imbalance was fairly soon remedied by the creation of a central equalization fund, which made it possible to distribute resources fairly. In December 1936, a trade-union assembly was held in Valencia, where it was decided to coordinate the various sectors of production into a general organic plan, which would make it possible to avoid harmful competition and the dissipation of effort.

At this point the trade unions undertook the systematic reorganization of whole trades, closing down hundreds of small enterprises and concentrating production in those that had the best equipment. For instance: in Catalonia foundaries were reduced from over 70 to 24, tanneries from 71 to 40, glass works from about 100 to about 30. However, industrial centralization under trade-union control could not be developed as rapidly and completely as the anarcho-syndicalist planners would have wished. Why was this? Because the Stalinists and reformists opposed the appropriation of the property of the middle class and showed scrupulous respect for the private sector.

In the other industrial centers of Republican Spain the Catalonian socialization decree was not in force and collectivizations were not so frequent as in Catalonia; however, private enterprises were often endowed with workers' control committees, as was the case in the Asturias.

Industrial self-management was, on the whole, as successful as agricultural self-management had been. Observers at first hand were full of praise, especially with regard to the excellent working of urban public services under self-management. Some factories, if not all, were managed in a remarkable fashion. Socialized industry made a major contribution to the war against fascism. The few arms factories built in Spain before 1936 had been set up outside Catalonia: the employers, in fact, were afraid of the Catalonian proletariat. In the Barcelona region, therefore, it was necessary to convert factories in great haste so that they might serve the defense of the Republic. Workers and technicians competed with each other in enthusiasm and initiative, and very soon war materiel made mainly in Catalonia was arriving at the front. No less effort was put into the manufacture of chemical products essential for war purposes. Socialized industry went ahead equally fast in the field of civilian requirements; for the first time the conversion of textile fibers was undertaken in Spain, and hemp, esparto, rice straw, and cellulose were processed.

SELF-MANAGEMENT UNDERMINED

In the meanwhile, credit and foreign trade had remained in the hands of the private sector because the bourgeois Republican government wished it so. It is true that the State controlled the banks, but it took care not to place them under self-management. Many collectives were short of working capital and had to live on the available funds taken over at the time of the July 1936 Revolution. Consequently they had to meet their day-to-day needs by chance acquisitions such as the seizure of jewelry and precious objects belonging to churches, convents, or Franco supporters who had fled. The CNT had proposed the creation of a "confederal bank" to finance self-management. But it was utopian to try to compete with private finance capital which had not been socialized. The only solution would have been to put all finance capital into the hands of the organized proletariat; but the CNT was imprisoned in the Popular Front, and dared not go as far as that.

The major obstacle, however, was the increasingly open hostility to self-management manifested by the various political general staffs of Republican Spain. It was charged with breaking the "united front" between the working class and the small bourgeoisie, and hence "playing the game" of the fascist enemy. (Its detractors went so far as to refuse arms to the libertarian vanguard which, on the Aragon front, was reduced to facing the fascist machine guns with naked hands—and then being reproached for its "inactivity.")

It was the Stalinist minister of agriculture, Vicente Uribe, who had established the decree of October 7, 1936, which legalized part of the rural collectivizations. Appearances to the contrary, he was imbued with an anti-collectivist spirit and hoped to demoralize the peasants living in socialized groups. The validation of collectivizations was subjected to very rigid and complicated juridical regulations. The collectives were obliged to adhere to an extremely strict time limit, and those which had not been legalized on the due date were automatically placed outside the law and their land made liable to being restored to the previous owners.

Uribe discouraged the peasants from joining the collectives and fomented discontent against them. In December 1936 he made a speech directed to the individualist small proprietors, declaring that the guns of the Communist Party and the government were at their disposal. He gave them imported fertilizer which he was refusing to the collectives. Together with his Stalinist colleague, Juan Comorera, in charge of the economy of Catalonia, he brought the small- and medium-scale landowners together into a reactionary union, subsequently adding the traders and even some owners of large estates disguised as smallholders. They took the organization of food supplies for Barcelona away from the workers' unions and handed it over to private trade.

Finally, when the advance guard of the Revolution in Barcelona had been crushed in May 1937,* the coalition government went so far as to liquidate agricultural self-management by military means. On the pretext that it had remained "outside the current of centralization," the Aragon "regional defense council" was dissolved by a decree of August 10, 1937. Its founder, Joaquín Ascaso, was charged with "selling jewelry," which was actually an attempt to get funds for the collectives. Soon after this, the 11th Mobile Division of Commander Lister (a Stalinist), supported by tanks, went into action against the collectives. Aragon was invaded like an enemy country, those in charge of socialized enterprises were arrested, their premises occupied, then closed; management committees were dissolved, communal shops emptied, furniture broken up, and flocks disbanded. The Communist press denounced "the crimes of forced collectivization." Thirty percent of the Aragon collectives were completely destroyed.

Even by this brutality, however, Stalinism was not generally successful in forcing the peasants of Aragon to become private owners. Peasants had been forced at pistol point to sign deeds of ownership, but as soon as the Lister Division had gone, these were

* This refers to the time when the POUM (Partido Obrero Unido Marxista) together with rank-and-file anarchists came into armed conflict with the police and were defeated and crushed. (Translator's note.)

destroyed and the collectives rebuilt. As G. Munis, the Spanish Trotskyist, wrote: "This was one of the most inspiring episodes of the Spanish Revolution. The peasants reaffirmed their socialist beliefs in spite of governmental terror and the economic boycott to which they were subjected."

There was another, less heroic, reason for the restoration of the Aragon collectives: the Communist Party had realized, after the event, that it had injured the life force of the rural economy, endangered the crops from lack of manpower, demoralized the fighters on the Aragon front, and dangerously reinforced the middle class of landed proprietors. The Party, therefore, tried to repair the damage it had itself done, and to revive some of the collectives. The new collectives, however, never regained the extent or quality of land of their predecessors, nor the original manpower, since many militants had been imprisoned or had sought shelter from persecution in the anarchist divisions at the front.

Republicans carried out armed attacks of the same kind against agricultural self-management in the Levant, in Castile, and in the provinces of Huesca and Teruel. However, it survived, by hook or by crook, in many areas which had not yet fallen into the hands of the Franco troops, especially in the Levant.

The ambiguous attitude, to put it mildly, of the Valencia government to rural socialism contributed to the defeat of the Spanish Republic: the poor peasants were not always clearly aware that it was in their interests to fight for the Republic.

In spite of its successes, industrial self-management was sabotaged by the administrative bureaucracy and the authoritarian socialists. The radio and press launched a formidable preparatory campaign of denigration and calumny, questioning the honesty of the factory management councils. The Republican central government refused to grant any credit to Catalonian self-management even when the libertarian minister of the Catalonian economy, Fabregas, offered the billion pesetas of savings bank deposits as security. In June 1937, the Stalinist Comorera took over the portfolio of the economy, and deprived the self-managed factories of raw materials which he lavished on the private sector. He also failed to deliver to the socialist enterprises supplies which had been ordered for them by the Catalan administration.

The central government had a stranglehold over the collectives; the nationalization of transport made it possible for it to supply some and cut off all deliveries to others. Moreover, it imported Republican army uniforms instead of turning to the Catalonian textile collectives. On August 22, 1937, it passed a decree suspending the application of the Catalonian October 1936 socialization decree to the metal and mining industries. This was done on the pretext of the necessities of national defense; and the Catalonian decree was said to be "contrary to the spirit of the Constitution." Foremen and managers who had been driven out by self-management, or rather, those who had been unwilling to accept technical posts in the self-managed enterprises, were brought back, full of a desire for revenge.

The end came with the decree of August 11, 1938, which militarized all war industries under the control of the Ministry of War Supplies. An overblown and ill-behaved bureaucracy invaded the factories—a swarm of inspectors and directors who owed their position solely to their political affiliations, in particular to their recent membership in the Stalinist Communist Party. The workers became demoralized as they saw themselves deprived of control over enterprises which they had created from scratch during the first critical months of the war, and production suffered in consequence.

In other branches, Catalan industrial self-management survived until the Spanish Republic was crushed. It was slowed down, however, for industry had lost its main outlets and there was a shortage of raw materials, the government having cut off the credit necessary to purchase them.

To sum up, the newborn Spanish collectives were immediately forced into the strait jacket of a war carried on by classic military methods, in the name of which the Republic clipped the wings of its own vanguard and compromised with reaction at home.

The lesson which the collectives have left behind them, however, is a stimulating one. In 1938 Emma Goldman was inspired to praise them thus: "The collectivization of land and industry shines out as the greatest achievement of any revolutionary period. Even if Franco were to win and the Spanish anarchists were to be exterminated, the idea they have launched will live on." On July 21,

1937, Federica Montseny made a speech in Barcelona in which she clearly posed the alternatives: "On the one hand, the supporters of authority and the totalitarian State, of a state-directed economy, of a form of social organization which militarizes all men and converts the State into one huge employer, one huge entrepreneur; on the other hand, the operation of mines, fields, factories and workshops, by the working class itself, organized in trade-union federations." This was the dilemma of the Spanish Revolution, but in the near future it may become that of socialism the world over.

By Way of Conclusion

The defeat of the Spanish Revolution deprived anarchism of its only foothold in the world. It came out of this trial crushed, dispersed, and, to some extent, discredited. History condemned it severely and, in certain respects, unjustly. It was not in fact, or at any rate alone, responsible for the victory of the Franco forces. What remained from the experience of the rural and industrial collectives, set up in tragically unfavorable conditions, was on the whole to their credit. This experience was, however, underestimated, calumniated, and denied recognition. Authoritarian socialism had at last got rid of undesirable libertarian competition and, for years, remained master of the field. For a time it seemed as though state socialism was to be justified by the military victory of the U.S.S.R. against Nazism in 1945 and by undeniable, and even imposing, successes in the technical field.

However, the very excesses of this system soon began to generate their own negation. They engendered the idea that paralyzing state centralization should be loosened up, that production units should have more autonomy, that workers would do more and better work if they had some say in the management of enterprises. What medicine calls "antibodies" were generated in one of the countries brought into servitude by Stalin. Tito's Yugoslavia freed itself from the too heavy yoke which was making it into a sort of colony. It then proceeded to re-evaluate the dogmas which could now so clearly be seen as anti-economic. It went back to school under the masters of the past, discovering and discreetly reading Proudhon. It bubbled in anticipation. It explored the too-little-known libertarian areas of thinking in the works of Marx and Lenin. Among

144

other things it dug out the concept of the withering away of the State, which had not, it is true, been altogether eliminated from the political vocabulary, but had certainly become no more than a ritual formula quite empty of substance. Going back to the short period during which Bolshevism had identified itself with proletarian democracy from below, with the soviets, Yugoslavia gleaned a word which had been enunciated by the leaders of the October Revolution and then quickly forgotten: self-management. Attention was also turned to the embryonic factory councils which had arisen at the same time, through revolutionary contagion, in Germany and Italy and, much later, Hungary. As reported in the French review *Arguments* by the Italian, Roberto Guiducci, the question arose whether "the idea of the councils, which had been suppressed by Stalinism for obvious reasons," could not "be taken up again in modern terms."

When Algeria was decolonized and became independent its new leaders sought to institutionalize the spontaneous occupations of abandoned European property by peasants and workers. They drew their inspiration from the Yugoslav precedent and took its legislation in this matter as a model.

If its wings are not clipped, self-management is undoubtedly an institution with democratic, even libertarian tendencies. Following the example of the Spanish collectives of 1936–1937, self-management seeks to place the economy under the management of the producers themselves. To this end a three-tier workers' representation is set up in each enterprise, by means of elections: the sovereign general assembly; the workers' council, a smaller deliberative body; and, finally, the management committee, which is the executive organ. The legislation provides certain safeguards against the threat of bureaucratization: representatives cannot stand for re-election too often, must be directly involved in production, etc. In Yugoslavia the workers can be consulted by referendum as an alternative to general assemblies, while in very large enterprises general assemblies take place in work sections.

Both in Yugoslavia and in Algeria, at least in theory, or as a promise for the future, great importance is attributed to the commune, and much is made of the fact that self-managing workers will be represented there. In theory, again, the management of public affairs should tend to become decentralized, and to be carried out more and more at the local level.

These good intentions are far from being carried out in practice. In these countries self-management is coming into being in the framework of a dictatorial, military, police state whose skeleton is formed by a single party. At the helm there is an authoritarian and paternalistic authority which is beyond control and above criticism. The authoritarian principles of the political administration and the libertarian principles of the management of the economy are thus quite incompatible.

Moreover, a certain degree of bureaucratization tends to show itself even within the enterprises, in spite of the precautions of the legislators. The majority of the workers are not yet mature enough to participate effectively in self-management. They lack education and technical knowledge, have not got rid of the old wage-earning mentality, and too willingly put all their powers into the hands of their delegates. This enables a small minority to be the real managers of the enterprise, to arrogate to themselves all sorts of privileges and do exactly as they like. They also perpetuate themselves in directorial positions, governing without control from below, losing contact with reality and cutting themselves off from the rank-and-file workers, whom they often treat with arrogance and contempt. All this demoralizes the workers and turns them against self-management. Finally, state control is often exercised so indiscreetly and so oppressively that the "self-managers" do not really manage at all. The state appoints directors to the organs of self-management without much caring whether the latter agree or not, although, according to the law, they should be consulted. These bureaucrats often interfere excessively in management, and sometimes behave in the same arbitrary way as the former employers. In very large Yugoslav enterprises directors are nominated entirely by the State; these posts are handed out to his old guard by Marshall Tito.

Moreover, Yugoslavian self-management is extremely dependent on the State for finance. It lives on credits accorded to it by the State and is free to dispose of only a small part of its profits, the rest being paid to the treasury in the form of a tax. Revenue derived from the self-management sector is used by the State not only to develop the backward sectors of the economy, which is no more than just, but also to pay for the heavily bureaucratized government apparatus, the army, the police forces, and for prestige expenditure, which is sometimes quite excessive. When the members of self-managed enterprises are inadequately paid, this blunts the enthusiasm for self-management and is in conflict with its principles.

The freedom of action of each enterprise, moreover, is fairly strictly limited, since it is subject to the economic plans of the central authority, which are drawn up arbitrarily without consultation of the rank and file. In Algeria the self-managed enterprises are also obliged to cede to the State the commercial handling of a considerable portion of their products. In addition, they are placed under the supervision of "organs of tutelage," which are supposed to supply disinterested technical and bookkeeping assistance but, in practice, tend to replace the organs of self-management and take over their functions.

In general, the bureaucracy of the totalitarian State is unsympathetic to the claims of self-management to autonomy. As Proudhon foresaw, it finds it hard to tolerate any authority external to itself. It dislikes socialization and longs for nationalization, that is to say, the direct management by officials of the State. Its object is to infringe upon self-management, reduce its powers, and in fact absorb it.

The single party is no less suspicious of self-management, and likewise finds it hard to tolerate a rival. If it embraces self-management, it does so to stifle it more effectively. The party has cells in most of the enterprises and is strongly tempted to take part in management, to duplicate the organs elected by the workers or reduce them to the role of docile instruments, by falsifying elections and setting out lists of candidates in advance. The party tries to induce the workers' councils to endorse decisions already taken in advance, and to manipulate and shape the national congresses of the workers.

Some enterprises under self-management react to authoritarian and centralizing tendencies by becoming isolationist, behaving as though they were an association of small proprietors, and trying to operate for the sole benefit of the workers involved. They tend to reduce their manpower so as to divide the cake into larger portions. They also seek to produce a little of everything instead of specializing. They devote time and energy to getting around plans or regulations designed to serve the interests of the community as a whole. In Yugoslavia free competition between enterprises has been allowed, both as a stimulant and to protect the consumer, but in practice the tendency to autonomy has led to flagrant inequalities output and to economic irrationalities.

Thus self-management itself incorporates a pendulum-like movement which makes it swing constantly between two extremes: excessive autonomy or excessive centralization; authority or anarchy; control from below or control from above. Through the years Yugoslavia, in particular, has corrected centralization by autonomy, then autonomy by centralization, constantly remodeling its institutions without so far successfully attaining a "happy medium."

Most of the weaknesses of self-management could be avoided or corrected if there were an authentic trade-union movement, independent of authority and of the single party, springing from the workers themselves and at the same time organizing them, and animated by the spirit characteristic of Spanish anarcho-syndicalism. In Yugoslavia and in Algeria, however, trade unionism is either subsidiary or supernumerary, or is subject to the State, to the single party. It cannot, therefore, adequately fulfill the task of conciliator between autonomy and centralization which it should undertake, and could perform much better than totalitarian political organs. In fact, a trade unionism which genuinely issued from the workers, who saw in it their own reflection, would be the most effective organ for harmonizing the centrifugal and centripetal forces, for "creating an equilibrium" as Proudhon put it, between the contradictions of self-management.

The picture, however, must not be seen as entirely black. Self-management certainly has powerful and tenacious opponents, who have not given up hope of making it fail. But it has, in fact, shown itself quite dynamic in the countries where experiments are being carried on. It has opened up new perspectives for the workers and restored to them some pleasure in their work. It has opened their minds to the rudiments of authentic socialism, which involves the progressive disappearance of wages, the disalienation of the producer who will become a free and self-determining being. Self-management has in this way increased productivity and registered considerable positive results, even during the trials and errors of the initial period.

From rather too far away, small circles of anarchists follow the development of Yugoslav and Algerian self-management with a mixture of sympathy and disbelief. They feel that it is bringing some fragments of their ideal into reality, but the experiment is not developing along the idealistic lines foreseen by libertarian communism. On the contrary it is being tried in an authoritarian framework which is repugnant to anarchism. There is no doubt that this framework makes self-management fragile: there is always a danger that it will be devoured by the cancer of authoritarianism. However, a close and unprejudiced look at self-management seems to reveal rather encouraging signs.

In Yugoslavia self-management is a factor favoring the democratization of the regime. It has created a healthier basis for recruitment in working-class circles. The party is beginning to act as an inspiration rather than a director, its cadres are becoming better spokesmen for the masses, more sensitive to their problems and aspirations. As Albert Meister, a young Swiss sociologist who set himself the task of studying this phenomenon on the spot, comments, self-management contains a "democratic virus" which, in the long run, invades the single party itself. He regards it as a "tonic." It welds the lower party echelons to the working masses. This development is so clear that it is bringing Yugoslav theoreticians to use language which would not disgrace a libertarian. For example, one of them, Stane Kavcic, states: "In future the striking force of socialism in Yugoslavia cannot be a political party and the State acting from the top down, but the people, the citizens, with constitutional rights which enable them to act from the base up." He continues bravely that self-management is increasingly loosening up "the rigid discipline and subordination which are characteristic of all political parties."

The trend is not so clear in Algeria, for the experiment is of more recent origin and still in danger of being called into question. A clue may be found in the fact that at the end of 1964, Hocine

Zahouane, then head of orientation of the National Liberation Front, publicly condemned the tendency of the "organs of guidance" to place themselves above the members of the self-management groups and to adopt an authoritarian attitude toward them. He went on: "When this happens, socialism no longer exists. There remains only a change in the form of exploitation of the workers." This official concluded by asking that the producers "should be truly masters of their production" and no longer be "manipulated for ends which are foreign to socialism." It must be admitted that Hocine Zahouane has since been removed from office by a military *coup d'état* and has become the leading spirit of a clandestine socialist opposition. He is for the time being* in compulsory residence in a torrid area of the Sahara.

To sum up, self-management meets with all kinds of difficulties and contradictions, yet, even now, it appears in practice to have the merit of enabling the masses to pass through an apprenticeship in direct democracy acting from the bottom upward; the merit of developing, encouraging, and stimulating their free initiative, of imbuing them with a sense of responsibility instead of perpetuating age-old habits of passivity, submission, and the inferiority complex left to them by past oppression, as is the case under state communism. This apprenticeship is sometimes laborious, progresses rather slowly, loads society with extra burdens and may, possibly, be carried out only at the cost of some "disorder." Many observers think, however, that these difficulties, delays, extra burdens, and growing pains are less harmful than the false order, the false luster, the false "efficiency" of state communism which reduces man to nothing, kills the initiative of the people, paralyzes production, and, in spite of material advances obtained at a high price, discredits the very idea of socialism.

The U.S.S.R. itself is re-evaluating its methods of economic management, and will continue to do so unless the present tendency to liberalization is cancelled by a regression to authoritarianism. Before he fell, on October 15, 1964, Khrushchev seemed to have understood, however timidly and belatedly, the need for in-

---

* As of July 1969.

dustrial decentralization. In December 1964 *Pravda* published a long article entitled "The State of the Whole People" which sought to define the changes of structure that differentiate the form of State "said to be of the whole people" from that of the "dictatorship of the proletariat"; namely, progress toward democratization, participation of the masses in the direction of society through self-management, and the revitalization of the soviets, the trade unions, etc.

The French daily *Le Monde* of February 16, 1965, published an article by Michel Tatu, entitled "A Major Problem: The Liberation of the Economy," exposing the most serious evils "affecting the whole Soviet bureaucratic machine, especially the economy." The high technical level this economy has attained makes the rule of bureaucracy over management even more unacceptable. As things are at present, directors of enterprises cannot make decisions on any subject without referring to at least one office, and more often to half a dozen. "No one disputes the remarkable technical, scientific, and economic progress which has been made in thirty years of Stalinist planning. The result, however, is precisely that this economy is now in the class of developed economies, and that the old structures which enabled it to reach this level are now totally, and ever more alarmingly, unsuitable." "Much more would be needed than detailed reforms; a spectacular change of thought and method, a sort of new de-Stalinization would be required to bring to an end the enormous inertia which permeates the machine at every level." As Ernest Mandel has pointed out, however, in an article in the French review *Les Temps Modernes*, decentralization cannot stop at giving autonomy to the directors of enterprises, it must lead to real workers' self-management.

The late Georges Gurvitch, a left-wing sociologist, came to a similar conclusion. He considers that tendencies to decentralization and workers' self-management have only just begun in the U.S.S.R., and that their success would show "that Proudhon was more right than one might have thought."

In Cuba the late state socialist Che Guevara had to quit the direction of industry, which he had run unsuccessfully owing to overcentralization. In *Cuba: Socialism and Development*, René Dumont, a French specialist in the Castro economy, deplores its "hypercentralization" and bureaucratization. He particularly emphasized the "authoritarian" errors of a ministerial department which tries to manage the factories itself and ends up with exactly the opposite results: "By trying to bring about a strongly centralized organization one ends up in practice . . . by letting any kind of thing be done, because one cannot maintain control over what is essential." He makes the same criticism of the state monopoly of distribution: the paralysis which it produces could have been avoided "if each production unit had preserved the function of supplying itself directly." "Cuba is beginning all over again the useless cycle of economic errors of the socialist countries," a Polish colleague in a very good position to know confided to René Dumont. The author concludes by abjuring the Cuban regime to turn to autonomous production units and, in agriculture, to federations of small farm-production cooperatives. He is not afraid to give the remedy a name, self-management, which could perfectly well be reconciled with planning. Unfortunately, the voice of René Dumont has not yet been heard in Havana.

The libertarian idea has recently come out of the shadow to which its detractors had relegated it. In a large part of the world the man of today has been the guinea pig of state communism, and is only now emerging, reeling, from the experience. Suddenly he is turning, with lively curiosity and often with profit, to the rough drafts for a new self-management society which the pioneers of anarchism were putting forward in the last century. He is not swallowing them whole, of course, but drawing lessons from them, and inspiration to try to complete the task presented by the second half of this century: to break the fetters, both economic and political, of what has been too simply called "Stalinism"; and this, without renouncing the fundamental principles of socialism: on the contrary, thereby discovering—or rediscovering—the forms of a real, authentic socialism, that is to say, socialism combined with liberty.

Proudhon, in the midst of the 1848 Revolution, wisely thought that it would have been asking too much of his artisans to go, immediately, all the way to "anarchy." In default of this maximum program, he sketched out a minimum libertarian program: progres-

sive reduction in the power of the State, parallel development of
the power of the people from below, through what he called clubs,
and which the man of the twentieth century would call councils.
It seems to be the more or less conscious purpose of many contemporary socialists to seek out such a program.

Although a possibility of revival is thus opened up for anarchism,
it will not succeed in fully rehabilitating itself unless it is able
to belie, both in theory and in practice, the false interpretations to
which it has so long been subject. As we saw, in 1924 Joaquín
Maurin was impatient to finish with it in Spain, and suggested that
it would never be able to maintain itself except in a few "backward countries" where the masses would "cling" to it because they
are entirely without "socialist education," and have been "left to
their natural instincts." He concluded: "Any anarchist who suc-
ceeds in improving himself, in learning, and in seeing clearly, automatically ceases to be an anarchist."

The French historian of anarchism, Jean Maitron, simply confused "anarchy" and disorganization. A few years ago he imagined
that anarchism had died with the nineteenth century, for our
epoch is one of "plans, organization, and discipline." More recently
the British writer George Woodcock saw fit to accuse the anarchists
of being idealists swimming against the dominant current of
history, feeding on an idyllic vision of the future while clinging to
the most attractive features of a dying past. Another English
specialist on the subject, James Joll, insists that the anarchists are
out-of-date, for their ideas are opposed to the development of
large-scale industry, to mass production and consumption, and
depend on a retrograde romantic vision of an idealized society of
artisans and peasants, and on a total rejection of the realities of
the twentieth century and of economic organization.*

In the preceding pages I have tried to show that this is not a
true picture of anarchism. Bakunin's works best express the nature
of constructive anarchism, which depends on organization, on self-
discipline, on integration, on federalist and noncoercive centraliza-

---

* James Joll recently wrote to the author that after reading this book he
had to some extent revised his views.

tion. It rests upon large-scale modern industry, up-to-date techniques, the modern proletariat, and internationalism on a world scale. In this regard it is of our times, and belongs to the twentieth century. It may well be state communism, and not anarchism, which is out of step with the needs of the contemporary world.

In 1924 Joaquín Maurin reluctantly admitted that throughout the history of anarchism "symptoms of decline" had been "followed by sudden revival." The future may show that only in this reluctant admission was the Spanish Marxist a good prophet.

Postscript: May 1968

It is some years since I first thought I had observed the beginning of a libertarian revolt among the youth of France. I was among those who watched with interest and, I must admit, with sympathy, the antics of young workers in conflict with society, at odds with the police and with all adults: the famous "black jackets," the organized gangs of the working-class areas.

Apart from these antisocial young people, I observed that our youth, in general, had no allegiance to anyone. Its obvious skepticism was neither detachment nor dilettantism, still less nihilism, but a comprehensive rejection of the false values of all its elders, be they bourgeois enamored of hierarchy and authority, or Stalinists, new Jesuits, obeying blindly the blindly obedient.

In 1958, in a debate on youth on the French radio I stated: "Socialism is still alive in the hearts of the young but, if it is to attract them, it must break with the tragic terrors of Stalinism, it must appear in libertarian guise." The following year I published a collection of essays entitled *Jeunesse du Socialisme Libertaire,** and prefaced it with the following dedication to youth:

"I dedicate these essays to you, youth of today.

"I know that you turn your back on ideologies and 'isms,' which have been made hollow by the failures of your elders. I know that you are deeply suspicious (and alas with much justification) about everything connected with 'politics.' I know that the grand old men who thought about the problem of society in the nineteenth century seem old bores to you. I know that you are justly skeptical of 'socialism,' which has been so often betrayed, so

---

* (Libertarian Socialist Youth), Paris, 1969.

brazenly botched up by its supporters. In replies made to an inquiry by the magazine *Nouvelle Vague* you gave the answer: 'A socialist future is not desirable because of the absolute subordination of the individual to a political idea, to the State.'

"You tell us that what puts you off about socialism is not the perspective of ending the oppression of man by man, it is 'the bureaucrats and the purges.'

"In other words you would desire socialism if it were authentic. The majority of you have a very strong feeling against social injustice and there are many among you who are aware that 'capitalism is condemned.' Moreover, you are passionately attached to liberty and one of your spokesmen writes that 'French youth is more and more anarchist.' You are libertarian socialists without knowing it. In contrast to the out-of-date, bankrupt, authoritarian, and totalitarian nature of Jacobin socialism, libertarian socialism bears the sign of youth. Not only because it is the secret of the future, the only possible rational and human substitute for an economic regime condemned by history, but also because it corresponds to the deepest, though often confused, aspirations of the youth of today. And without your agreement and participation it would be vain to try to reconstruct the world.

"One of these young people wrote 'I think I shall see this civilization collapse in my lifetime.' It is my modest wish to live long enough to witness and take part in this gigantic cleanup with you, youth. I hope that the case against false socialism presented in this work may suggest to you a few of the materials with which you will build a more just and free society with a new enthusiasm from which skepticism has disappeared."

The revolution of May 1968 in France fully confirmed this prediction. It was a great sweeping out of cobwebs. It was carried out by youth, not only students, but with working-class youth through the solidarity of their age and their common alienation. At the university as well as in the factory and trade union, dictatorship of the adults was challenged: the masters in the universities, the employers in the factories, and the bosses in the trade unions. More, it was profoundly shaken. And this unexpected explosion burst like a thunderclap, contagious and devastating, and was very largely libertarian socialist in character.

It was based upon a critique not only of bourgeois society but of post-Stalinist communism which had been becoming more and more acute in university circles. It was stimulated by the denunciation expressed in *La Misère en Milieu Etudiant** by a small group of "situationists," and it was inspired by the student rebellion in various countries, especially Germany.

It armed itself with direct action, purposeful illegality, the occupation of places of work: it was not afraid to meet the violence of the forces of repression by revolutionary violence; it put everything in question, all accepted ideas, all existing structures; it repudiated the professorial monologue as much as the authoritarianism of the employers; it rejected the cult of personality and insisted on anonymity and collectivity; in a few weeks it passed through a lightning apprenticeship in direct democracy, in the dialogue of a thousand voices, in the communication of all with all.

It drank greedily from the fountain of liberty. In all its meetings and forums of all kinds every individual was given the right to express himself fully. The public square was transformed into an amphitheater, for the traffic was stopped and the debaters seated on the pavement, the strategy of the future war of the streets discussed openly, fully, and at length. Anyone could come into the revolutionary beehive in the court, the corridors, and landings of the Sorbonne. There, every revolutionary tendency without exception could display and sell its literature.

The libertarians took advantage of this situation of freedom to abandon their former insularity. They fought side by side with the revolutionary Marxists of authoritarian tendency, almost without animosity on either side, temporarily forgetting the frictions of the past. The black flag flew alongside the red flag, without competition or conflict, at least during the sharpest phase of the struggle when everything was subordinated to fraternal unity against the common enemy.

---

* "Wretched Conditions of Student Life"—title of a pamphlet published in France in 1967 by students of the University of Strasbourg.

All authority was repudiated or even derided. The myth of the providential old man of the Elysée was not so much undermined by serious argument as blown sky high by caricature and satire. The parliamentary talk-shop was negated by the mortal weapon of indifference: one of the long marches of the students through the capital happened to pass in front of the Palais Bourbon without even condescending to notice its existence.

One magic word echoed through the glorious weeks of May 1968, in both factory and university. It was the theme of innumerable debates, explanations, references to historical precedent, detailed and enthusiastic examinations of relevant contemporary experiences: it was *self-management*. The example of the Spanish collectivizations of 1936 aroused particularly keen interest. In the evenings workers came to the Sorbonne to learn about this new solution to the problem of society. When they went back to the workshops, discussions on this subject went on around the silent machines. Of course the revolution of May 1968 did not put self-management into practice, it stopped just short—one might even say: on the very brink. But the idea of self-management has become lodged in people's minds, and it will emerge again sooner or later.

Finally, this revolution so profoundly libertarian in spirit had the good fortune of finding a spokesman: a young Franco-German Jewish anarchist, aged twenty-three, Daniel Cohn-Bendit, who, with a group of friends, acted as a detonator and, when he was expelled from France, as the living symbol of the revolution. "Dany" is no anarchist theoretician; in the field of ideas his brother Gaby, a teacher at the Saint-Nazaire Lycée probably excels him in maturity and in learning. But Dany has more striking gifts than book-learning: he has libertarian fire in the highest degree. He showed himself to be a born agitator, a speaker of unusual power, direct, realistic, concrete, provocative, impressing people without demagogy or artificiality. Moreover, like a real libertarian, he refuses to play the leader and insists on remaining one militant among many. He was the moving spirit of the first student revolt in France, at the University of Nanterre and so, without premeditation, contributed to setting off the gigantic confrontation which shook the whole country. The bourgeoisie would not forgive him

for it, still less the Stalinists, whom he regarded as "scoundrels."
They would both be wrong to think that they are rid of him: it
does not matter whether he is absent or present,* he will always be
at their heels.

One last word. This short book which is now to be published in
the United States, in English, became a best-seller in its country
of origin during those weeks of regeneration, and has been, or is
going to be, translated into ten languages. The author claims no
credit for this; but is it not one of many signs of the renaissance of
anarchism in France and the world, through a revolution which has
only begun?

---

* Cohn-Bendit, being a German citizen, though born in France, was expelled from the country by the Gaullist regime (May 1968) and has not
since been allowed to return to France.

Bibliography

Anthologies
Guérin, Daniel. *Ni Dieu ni Maître: Histoire et Anthologie de l'anarch-isme.* 2 vols. Lausanne, 1969.
Horowitz, Irving L. *The Anarchists.* New York, 1964.
Krimerman, Leonard I., and Perry, Lewis. *Patterns of Anarchy.* New York, 1966.

General
Arvon, Henri. *L'Anarchisme.* Paris, 1951.
Berkman, Alexander. *The A.B.C. of Anarchist Communism.* London, 1942.
Goldman, Emma. *Anarchism and Other Essays.* New York, 1911.
Hamon, Augustin. *Psychologie de l'Anarchiste-Socialiste.* 1895.
———. *Le Socialisme et le Congrès de Londres.* 1897.
Joll, James. *The Anarchists.* Boston, 1964.
Maitron, Jean. *Histoire du Mouvement Anarchiste en France (1894–1914).* Paris, 1955.
Maximoff, G. P. *Constructive Anarchism.* Chicago, 1952.
Parsons, A. R., and others. *Anarchism: Its Philosophy and Scientific Basis.* Chicago, 1887.
Read, Herbert. *Anarchy and Order.* London, 1954.
———. *The Philosophy of Anarchism.* London, 1940.
Sergeant, Alain and Harmel, Claude. *Histoire de l'Anarchie.* Paris, 1949.
Woodcock, George. *Anarchism.* New York, 1962.
Zoccoli, Ettore. *L'Anarchia.* Turin, 1907.

Stirner
Arvon, Henri. *Aux Sources de l'Existentialisme: Max Stirner.* Paris, 1954.

Stirner, Max. *The Ego and Its Own*. New York, 1907.
————. *Kleinere Schriften*. Berlin, 1898.

Proudhon

Brogan, D. W. *Proudhon*. London, 1936.
Edwards, Stewart. *Selected Writings of P-J. Proudhon*. New York, 1969.
Gurvitch, Georges. *Proudhon*. Paris, 1965.
Proudhon, P.-J. *Carnets de P-J. Proudhon*. Paris, 1960.
————. *Manuel du Spéculateur à la Bourse*. Paris, 1852. 3rd enlarged edition, 1857.
————. *Oeuvres Complètes*. 26 vols. Paris, 1867–1870. New edition, Paris, 1938.
————. *Théorie de la Propriété*. 1865.
Woodcock, George. *Pierre-Joseph Proudhon*. London, 1956.

Bakunin

Bakounine, Michel. *Archives Bakounine*. 4 vols. Leiden, 1961–1965.
————. *Lettres à A. Herzen et à N. Ogareff, 1860–1870*. Edited by Michel Dragomanoff. 1896.
————. *La Liberté*. Paris, 1965.
————. *Oeuvres*. 6 vols. Paris, 1896–1914.
Bakunin, Michael. *God and the State*. Boston, 1893.
————. *Marxism, Freedom, and the State*. London, 1950.
Maximoff, G. P., ed. *The Political Philosophy of Bakunin: Scientific Anarchism*. Glencoe, Ill., 1953.
Nettlau, Max. *Michael Bakunin*. 3 vols. London, 1896–1900.
Pyziur, Eugene. *The Doctrine of Anarchism of M. A. Bakunin*. Milwaukee, 1955.

The First International

de Paepe, César. *De l'Organisation des Services Publics dans la Société Future*. Brussells, 1874.
————. *Mémoire du District de Courtelary*. Geneva, 1880.
Freymond, Jacques. *La Première Internationale*. 2 vols. Geneva, 1962.
Guillaume, James. *Idées sur l'Organisation Sociale*. 1876.
————. *L'Internationale: Documents et Souvenirs (1864–1878)*. 4 vols. Paris, 1905–1910.
Molnar, Miklos. *Le Déclin de la Première Internationale*. Geneva, 1963.

Stekl-off, G. M. *History of the First International.* London, 1928. Reprint, New York, 1968.

Commune of 1871

Bakounine, Michel. *La Commune de Paris et la Notion de l'Etat.* 1871.

Jellinek, Frank. *The Paris Commune.* New York, 1967.

Lefebvre, Henri. *La Proclamation de la Commune.* Paris, 1965.

Lissagary, P. O. *History of the Commune of 1871.* 1886. Reprint, New York, 1967.

Marx, Karl. *The Civil War in France.* New York, 1940.

Kropotkin

Berneri, Camillo. *Peter Kropotkin: His Federalist Ideas.* London, 1942.

Kropotkin, Peter. *The Conquest of Bread.* London, 1906. Reprint, New York, 1968.

———. *Ethics: Origin and Development.* New York, 1924. Reprint, New York, 1968.

———. *Fields, Factories, and Workshops.* London, 1899. Reprint, New York, 1968.

———. *Kropotkin's Revolutionary Pamphlets.* G. Roger N. Baldwin, ed. 1927. Reprint, New York, 1968.

———. *Memoirs of a Revolutionist.* 1899. Reprint, New York, 1968.

———. *Modern Science and Anarchism.* London, 1912.

———. *Mutual Aid: A Factor in Evolution.* London, 1904. Reprint, New York, 1955.

———. *The State: Its Historic Role.* London, 1898.

Woodcock, George and Avakumović, Ivan. *The Anarchist Prince: A Biography of Peter Kropotkin.* London, 1950.

Malatesta

Malatesta, Errico. *Anarchy.* London, 1942.

———. *Malatesta: His Life and Ideas.* London, 1965.

———. *Programme et Organisation de l'Association Internationale des Travailleurs.* Florence, 1884. Reprinted in *Studi Sociali,* Montevideo, May–November 1934.

Syndicalism

Besnard, Pierre. *Les Syndicats Ouvriers et la Révolution Sociale.* Paris, 1930.

Monatte, Pierre. *Trois Scissions Syndicales.* Paris, 1958.

Pataud, E. and Pouget, E. *Syndicalism and Co-operative Commonwealth.* Oxford, 1913.

Pelloutier, Fernand. "L'Anarchisme et les Syndicats Ouvriers" in *Les Temps Nouveau,* November 1895.

———. *Histoire des Bourses du Travail.* Paris, 1902.

Pouget, Emile. *Ad Memoriam.* 1931.

———. *Le Parti du Travail.* Reprint, 1931.

———. *Le Syndicat.* Nd.

Rocker, Rudolph. *Anarcho-Syndicalism.* London, 1938.

Russian Revolution

Archinoff, Pierre. *L'Histoire du Mouvement Makhnoviste.* Paris, 1928.

Berkman, Alexander. *The Anti-Climax.* Berlin, 1925.

———. *The Bolshevik Myth (Diary, 1920–1921).* New York, 1925.

———. *The Kronstadt Rebellion.* Berlin, 1922.

———. *La Révolution Russe et le Parti Communiste.* Paris, 1921.

———. *The Russian Tragedy.* Berlin, 1922.

Deutscher, Isaac. *Trotsky.* 3 vols. New York, 1954–1959.

Fabbri, Luigi. *Dittatura e Rivoluzione.* Milan, 1921.

Fedeli, Ugo. *Dalla Insurrezione dei Contadini in Ucraina alla Rivolta di Cronstadt.* Milan, 1950.

Goldman, Emma. *Les Bolcheviks et la Révolution Russe.* Berlin, 1922.

———. *Living My Life.* New York, 1931.

———. *My Disillusionment in Russia.* New York, 1923.

———. *My Further Disillusionment with Russia.* New York, 1923.

———. *Trotsky Protests Too Much.* New York, 1938.

Kollantay, Alexandra. *L'Opposition Ouvière.* 1921. Reissued in *Socialisme ou Barbarie,* No. 35, 1964.

Kubanin, M. *Makhnoshchina.* Leningrad, nd.

Lenin, V. I. *Left-Wing Communism: An Infantile Disorder.* New York, 1940.

———. *State and Revolution.* New York, 1932.

Leval, Gaston. *Le Chemin du Socialisme, les Débuts de la Crise Communiste Bolchevique.* Geneva, 1958.

———. "Choses de Russie," in *Le Libertaire,* November 11–18, 1921.

Makhno, Nestor. *La Révolution Russe en Ukraine.* Paris, 1927.

Maximoff, G. P. *The Guillotine at Work: Twenty Years of Terror in Russia.* Chicago, 1940.

Mett, Ida. *La Commune de Cronstadt.* 1938. Reprint, 1948.

Mett, Ida. *The Kronstadt Commune.* Solidarity Pamphlet No. 27, November 1927.

Pankratova, A. *Les Comités d'Usine de Russie.* Moscow, 1923.

Rocker, Rudolph. *Die Bankrotte des Russischen Staatskommunismus.* Berlin, 1921.

Sadoul, Georges. *Notes sur la Révolution Bolchevique.* Paris, 1919.

Serge, Victor. *L'An I de la Révolution Russe.* Reprint, 1965.

——. *Memoirs of a Revolutionary, 1901–1941.* Reprint, New York, 1967.

Shapiro, Léonard. *Les Bolcheviks et l'Opposition (1917–1922).* Paris, 1957.

Stepanov, I. *Du Contrôle Ouvrier à l'Administration Ouvrière.* Moscow, 1918.

Trotsky, Leon. *1905.* Reissued 1966 in French.

——. *History of the Russian Revolution.* New York, 1957.

Voline [Vsévolod Mikhailovitch Eichenbaum]. *The Unknown Revolution, 1917–1921.* New York, 1955.

Yartciuk, E. *Kronstadt.* Barcelona, 1930.

St. Anthony's Papers, No. 6. London, 1959. (On Kronstadt and Makhno.)

Councils

Gorter, Hermann. *Réponse à Lénine.* 1920. Reprint, 1930.

Gramsci, Antonio. *L'Ordine Nuovo (1919–1920).* 1954.

Masini, Pier Carlo. *Anarchici e Communisti nel Movimento dei Consigli.* Milan, 1954.

——. *Gli Anarchici Italiani e la Rivoluzione Russa.* 1962.

——. *Antonio Gramsci e l'Ordine Nuovo: Visti da un Libertario.* Leghorn, 1956.

Mühsam, Erich. *Auswahl.* Zurich, 1962.

Pannekoek, Anton. *Workers' Councils.* Reprint, Melbourne, 1950.

Spriano, Paolo. *L'Occupazione delle Fabbriche Settembre 1920.* Turin, 1964.

Spanish Revolution

Bolloten, Burnett. *The Grand Camouflage: The Communist Conspiracy in the Spanish Civil War.* New York, 1968.

Borkenau, Franz. *The Spanish Cockpit.* 1937. Reprint, Ann Arbor, 1965.

Brenan, Gerald. *The Spanish Labyrinth.* New York, 1943.

Broué Pierre and Témine, Emile. *La Révolution et la Guerre d'Espagne*. Paris, 1961.
Chomsky, Noam. "Objectivity and Liberal Scholarship" in *American Power and the New Mandarins*. New York, 1969.
Jellinek, Frank. *The Civil War in Spain*. London, 1938.
Leval, Gaston. *Ne Franco Ne Stalin*. Milan, 1952.
———. *Social Reconstruction in Spain*. London, 1938.
Maurin, Joaquín. *L'Anarcho-Syndicalisme en Espagne*. 1924.
———. *Révolution et Contre-Révolution en Espagne*. 1937.
Montseny, Federica. *Militant Anarchism and the Reality in Spain*. Glasgow, 1937.
Munis, G. *Jalones de Derrota*. Mexico, 1946.
Orwell, George. *Homage to Catalonia*. 1938. Reprint, Boston, 1955.
Peirats, José. *Los Anarquistas en la Crisis Politica Española*. Buenos Aires, 1964.
———. *La CNT en la Revolución Española*. 3 vols. Toulouse, 1951.
Puente, Dr. Isaac. *Il Comunismo Libertario*. 1932.
Rabassière, Henri. *Espagne Crueset Politique*. Nd.
Richards, Vernon. *Lessons of the Spanish Revolution*. London, 1953.
Santillan, D. A. de. *After the Revolution*. New York, 1937.
———. *La Revolución y la Guerra en España*. 1938.
Collectivités Anarchistes en Espagne Révolutionnaire in *Noir et Rouge* (March 1964) and *Collectivités Espagnoles* in *Noir et Rouge* (June 1965).

Contemporary Self-Management
Kavcic, Stane. *L'Autogestion en Yougoslavie*. 1961.
Meister, Albert. *Socialisme et Autogestion: L'Expérience Yougoslave*. 1964.
Les Tempes Modernes, June 1965.

Modern Reader Paperbacks

The Accumulation of Capital by Rosa Luxemburg $4.50
The Age of Imperialism by Harry Magdoff   1.95
The Alienation of Modern Man by Fritz Pappenheim   2.45
American Radicals, edited by Harvey Goldberg   3.45
The American Revolution: Pages from
   a Negro Worker's Notebook by James Boggs   1.65
The Black Man's Burden: The White Man in Africa from the
   Fifteenth Century to World War I by E. D. Morel   1.95
Capitalism and Underdevelopment in Latin America
   by Andre Gunder Frank   3.45
Capitalism as a System by Oliver C. Cox   3.95
Capitalism Yesterday and Today by Maurice Dobb   1.00
Caste, Class, and Race by Oliver C. Cox   4.50
The Communist Manifesto by Karl Marx & Friedrich Engels,
   including Engels' "Principles of Communism," and an
   essay, "The Communist Manifesto After 100 Years," by
   Paul M. Sweezy and Leo Huberman   1.45
Consciencism by Kwame Nkrumah   1.95
Cuba: Anatomy of a Revolution
   by Leo Huberman & Paul M. Sweezy   2.95
Dollar Diplomacy by Scott Nearing & Joseph Freeman   3.95
The Economic Transformation of Cuba by Edward Boorstein   3.45
The Empire of Oil by Harvey O'Connor   3.95
An Essay on Economic Growth and Planning
   by Maurice Dobb   1.95
The Explosion by Henri Lefebvre   2.25
Ghana: End of an Illusion
   by Bob Fitch & Mary Oppenheimer   1.75
The Great Tradition in English Literature
   by Annette Rubinstein (2 vols.)   7.95
The Growth of the Modern West Indies by Gordon K. Lewis   4.50
Guatemala: Occupied Country by Eduardo Galeano   2.25
Introduction to Socialism
   by Leo Huberman & Paul M. Sweezy   1.95

MONTHLY REVIEW

an independent socialist magazine
edited by Paul M. Sweezy and Harry Magdoff

Business Week: ". . . a brand of socialism that is thorough-going and tough-minded, drastic enough to provide the sharp break with the past that many left-wingers in the underdeveloped countries see as essential. At the same time they maintain a sturdy independence of both Moscow and Peking that appeals to neutralists. And their skill in manipulating the abstruse concepts of modern economics impresses would-be intellectuals. . . . Their analysis of the troubles of capitalism is just plausible enough to be disturbing."

Bertrand Russell: "Your journal has been of the greatest interest to me over a period of time. I am not a Marxist by any means as I have sought to show in critiques published in several books, but I recognize the power of much of your own analysis and where I disagree I find your journal valuable and of stimulating importance. I want to thank you for your work and to tell you of my appreciation of it."

The Wellesley Department of Economics: " . . . the leading Marxist intellectual (not Communist) economic journal published anywhere in the world, and is on our subscription list at the College library for good reasons."

Albert Einstein: "Clarity about the aims and problems of socialism is of greatest significance in our age of transition. . . . I consider the founding of this magazine to be an important public service." (In his article, "Why Socialism" in Vol. I, No. 1.)

DOMESTIC: $7 for one year, $12 for two years, $5 for one-year student subscription.

FOREIGN: $8 for one year, $14 for two years, $6 for one-year student subscription. (Subscription rates subject to change.)

116 West 14th Street, New York, New York 10011